FRONTLINE PROFIT MACHINE

**The Blueprint to Exploding Profits
with Your Existing Service and Sales Team**

Ziad Y. Khoury

SelectBooks, Inc.
New York

This edition published by SelectBooks, Inc.
For information address SelectBooks, Inc., New York, New York.

First Edition

ISBN 978-1-59079-186-8

Library of Congress Cataloging-in-Publication Data

Khoury, Ziad, 1967-
Frontline profit machine : the blueprint for exploding profits with your existing service and sales team / Ziad Khoury. -- 1st ed.
p. cm.
Includes index.
Summary: "Recommends a method to measure and improve salespersons' perfomance for increased revenue and business profit"--Provided by publisher.
ISBN 978-1-59079-186-8 (hardbound : alk. paper)
1. Selling. 2. Success in business. 3. Profit. 4. Point-of-sale systems
industry. I. Title.
HF5438.25.K48 2008
658.85--dc22
2008048835

Manufactured in the United States of America
10 9 8 7 6 5 4 3 2 1

DEDICATION

This book is dedicated to the memory of my father Joseph A. Khoury, who sacrificed so much to give my brother, my sister, and me the opportunities to further improve our lives. He taught us that it is always far better for people to think more highly of you as they get to know you—and that can only happen by doing the right things. My dad, who is my hero, always did the right thing, every time.

To my mother Georgette, whose unwavering belief and confidence always encourages me to achieve and do more.

To my brother Sean and my sister Mary, who are equally encouraging and absolutely terrific.

To my incredible family, and my biggest fans and supporters, my wife Lara and our two amazing children, Danielle and Joseph. I am a very lucky guy.

ACKNOWLEDGMENTS

I could not have produced this book without the help of so many. I want to thank the following individuals for their commitment and hard work, and most importantly, for their belief in the message of this book and for its execution in the marketplace.

Chris Brown, Khoury Group SVP, whose invaluable contributions are evident in many of the pages of this book. The outcome would not be what it is without his hard work. Chris is a committed member of the Khoury team whose leadership, high ethics, and continuous commitment help to shape the right environment within our own organization.

Ken Stellon, Khoury Group SVP, whose incredible creativity, thorough research, knowledge, energy, and enthusiasm helped shape the tone and message in this book. Further, Ken's contributions in running the business while I focused on this book were equally as valuable.

My gratitude goes to the entire team at The Khoury Group, led by Austin Johnson, Carole Wade, Mark Hart, Eddie Bartemes, and Lynda Fleming, whose work provided a significantly improved final outcome. Special thanks goes to my very first team member, Wende Rowland, for all that she does. Thank you to Bernie Sheehe for his hard work on the book.

This book would also not have been possible if it were not for the professional and dedicated contributions of the following individuals: My terrific agent and editor, Michael Roney, whose professionalism, hard work and commitment to getting it all right continues to add incredible value; Suzanne Miller, who meticulously laid out the pages of this book in great detail; my publisher Kenzi Sugihara, owner of SelectBooks, who stepped up with an offer to take on this book, and who has been terrific to work with; Maya Roney who contributed polished writing and editing; Nancy Sugihara, whose feedback enhanced the final product, and Mike Hinn whose agency, Knight, in Orlando, designed the cover.

I want to also thank some very special clients, mentors and friends who have helped shape my business and impact my life over the last 15 years: Jim Shapiro, who was my longest-standing client and is my very good friend; Sandy Miller, who gave us our biggest engagement in 1999 that helped transform our business; Don Lindo, my very good friend, big supporter, and the first to give me a Frontline sales management position; my partners and friends in my other businesses, Randy Harris, Omar Quddus, Bob Krebs, Matt Eggen and Phil Eggen, who all do outstanding work; my Young Presidents Organization forum members, Steve Griessel, Peter Kassabov, Hugh Caron, Mike Hinn, Ken Daley, Eddie Schatz and Michael Williamson, whose friendship and support is invaluable.

Finally, I want to thank every client we have ever had. I am forever grateful for anyone who has ever put a penny in our pocket.

Contents

Part Two: Understanding the
Khoury Performance Equation

Part Three: Implementing Your Plan for Exploding Profits

POWERING UP YOUR FRONTLINE PROFIT MACHINE

Consider the following truth:

For many companies a 5% to 10% improvement in top-line revenue can mean 100% improvement to the bottom line.

Now consider these very important facts that relate to your sales and your bottom-line:

- In most businesses you have very little control over your competitors, their pricing and their sometimes perplexing strategies. You have no control over the economy, or the litany of outside influences that affect the health of your business.

- What you do have control over is the performance of your own team, the environment you help create, and the people you invite into this environment to be part of your team. This is the "X" factor that you can put to use to create a 100% improvement in your bottom line.

And here's the kicker. For many businesses, improving the service and the sales ability of the Frontline—the team members that face your customers— usually provides the opportunity for the biggest upside impact for the organization.

Most basic or core revenue goes toward paying the bills. In a good month that revenue exceeds the amount needed to pay the bills and in a bad month it does not.

If your business plan is sound, your products and services are appealing, and you have good basic marketing, distribution and sales channels, you will generally bring in enough revenue to pay the bills and make some money.

But it's the *profitable* revenue, the revenue that puts you over the top (well past just paying the bills) that makes that P&L look oh-so-sweet. This is the *additional and incremental sales revenue* that your Frontline can produce.

The revenue that I am talking about flows from:

- Securing an up-sell at the front counter to the "luxury" suite that was sitting empty that night

- Adding one extra item to every third sale in your retail store

- Generating cross-sell referrals to the loan office, adding 20 extra loans that month for the branch

- Adding five points to the utilization and occupancy of your apartment complex, your car rental fleet or your airplanes, all of which you are paying for anyway

- Getting your sales team in the field to average one extra sale every other day

Whether your convenience store team member suggests one extra $4.99 12-pack special, or your real estate agent sells one extra million-dollar lot in your development, all of this happens by and through your Frontline.

⟳ Make Your Numbers Explode

Do you want to make a huge, dynamically positive impact on your customers, your company, your employees, and yourself? Then take the time to understand the significance of those numbers. Look at the difference in sales production between Joe, a top-10% producer, and Jim, who is average.

Joe sells 50% more than Jim does. What's that tell you about the potential? What's that tell you about the upside in your business?

Want to get really excited? What if you get more Jims to produce like Joe? Now apply some forecasting to what that number is, a number that represents the *incremental profitable revenue potential.*

Want to get incredibly excited? Now apply Joe's numbers and the potential revenue difference versus Sam, who is in the bottom 20%.

Want to drool over this upside? Understand that in most cases even the Joes—your top 10% producers—still have plenty of room for improvement.

Want to get started? Start with the Khoury Performance Equation, the KPE. Start by studying this book, studying the opportunity: how to sell it, how to identify the challenges and how to overcome them.

Take this knowledge and run with it. Great things are within your reach!

⟲ Beware of the Domi-"No" Effect

"Are you sure you don't want the five-year service agreement with that TV today?" your salesperson asks with a weak smile and a lot of desperation. "No thanks," you respond, with reluctance and a bit of annoyance. "I need to check with my wife." And you are not even married; you're simply *desperate* to get out of there!

We've all been in electronic stores where you can tell the salespeople have been told to "push" the service agreements. And the way you can tell they've been told to "push" it is because *you* "feel pushed" yourself.

Are these guys genuine, sincere, and really helpful? Do they build a good first impression and a good rapport? Do they ask you a few questions to really understand your needs? Do they know their products well? Have they built the value into what they are selling? Have they earned the right to sell you that plasma TV, much less the five-year warranty they are pushing?

Rarely! But if they did, you might find yourself a regular customer of that big- box electronics store. You may be less apt to shop for electronics based solely on price of the brand you are looking for, but instead base your shopping on the *experience* of becoming the proud owner of that plasma TV. If you understand its value better, you may also jump at the benefits and the peace of mind that comes with a five-year worry and hassle-free service plan.

When the sale is mechanical and insincere it sounds like this to the customer's ears: "I really just want more of your money." This obviously turns customers off and puts them into a "non-buying" mode.

While a poor salesperson may be lucky enough to sell the customer the TV he or she was really looking for, the salesperson is not likely to sell what the customer is *unsure* about, the five-year service plan.

If your salespeople are operating this way, they will hear the word "no" quite a bit. I have seen this scenario play out over and over again; if in a typical morning they have had had five customers say "no," a domi- "No" effect begins to take hold:

The customer says "no,"

- » which leads to a feeling of rejection on the part of the salesperson
- » which leads to a refusal from the salesperson to continue to sell consistently
- » which leads to another sales campaign crashing and burning
- » which leads managers to simply give up on this type of initiaive in the future

Sound familiar? Sales campaigns look much easier on paper. After all, you say, "How hard can it be? My twelve-year-old kid can sell this stuff!" But this is easier said than done. You need the comprehensive plan and proven system described in this book

➤ Pushing Them to "Do It" Will Not "Do It"

Whether you ask your staff to upgrade the ticket in your retail store by "pushing" socks with the order, or increase the travel package price by asking your contact center sales

> A "pushed" salesperson will usually "push" your customer, who then "pushes" back with a negative response. Before you know it, the entire sales initiative has been "pushed" off a cliff.

agents to "push" travel insurance, you are asking them to "push it" with nothing more than a directive to "do it" and maybe an incentive that you feel should drive them to "do it."

The executive or owner then asks what happened and the excuses start piling in:

- "Our customers already know exactly what they want"
- "Our customers are cheap"
- "Our customers are different"
  This one's a perennial favorite and a real classic!

➤ A "Simple Product" Does Not Make a "Simple Sale"

Whether you are upgrading or cross-selling a product, or converting a customer, in most cases the product or service that is being sold on the Frontline is relatively simple and unsophisticated. This gives management the misconception that a simple product requires a simple and unsophisticated sales and sales management process.

Nothing is further from the truth. This may sound familiar to the more experienced sales professional, but it can't be said enough: *products and services are sold by people, and people have feelings.* People are even more fragile when they are young and in entry-level sales positions.

They take the "no" personally and handle rejection poorly, paralyzing their ability to sell. The "pressure to sell" creates inevitable turnover and instability, making it even harder to attract and keep good people.

● You Need a Blueprint for Higher Profits

A successful sales campaign usually requires a marked change of behavior. It requires a plan, a *blueprint*. This blueprint entails creating the The Right Environment, bringing The Right Fit of employees into the environment, and then motivating them to undertake The Right Action. At the top of this list is the principle that you must effectively sell and service your valuable customers at the highest possible level.

Let's face it: You need a blueprint to build anything of value, anything of substance or anything that functions efficiently including a consistently high-performing sales organization.

Creating a high-performance culture in which selling is about "how" things are done on a daily basis requires much more effort, expertise, and focus than creating a flavor-of-the-month sales campaign.

Capitalizing on sales opportunities that exist in your business not only requires a blueprint, but one that can be customized and actually put into action. If you are a CEO, an executive, a small business owner or a manager who is trying to build a dynamic, service-based sales team, in other words, a Frontline Profit Machine , the blueprint you need is in this book. The Khoury Performance Equation is that blueprint.

● Your Personal "How to" System

This book provides a framework and an implementation plan to help you reach your performance potential. This will allow your customers to enjoy great benefits while experiencing immense satisfaction in choosing your best products or services. You'll quickly realize that *Frontline Profit Machine* is not completely made up of original and unique ideas, although you will find quite a few.

This book is uniquely powerful because it weaves existing and original ideas together into a workable framework. This framework has already revolutionized the Frontline sales process at companies such as Rocky Mountain Chocolate Factory and Budget Rent a Car in the United States and Canada, First Choice in Europe, and Sandals and Beaches Resorts in the Caribbean.

The ideas in this book are not merely conceptual. They have been battle-tested and fortified for over 15 years through our organization's work around the world. They have achieved sustainable proven results, even in the most difficult selling scenarios and environments.

If you embrace the guidance in this book, you will have a practical plan to achieve what all owners and managers want—happy customers, happy employees, and improved profits.

The only question you now need to ask yourself is: Do I want to operate a merely average-performing sales organization, or do I want to lead a thriving Frontline Profit Machine?

➲ The Khoury Performance Equation: An Overview

Defining a theoretical Frontline strategy for high profitability is *not a difficult thing to do.* Getting people to do it, and do it consistently, is.

That's where the KPE system comes in. It's a business blueprint designed to optimize sales and service performance through three primary areas of actionable focus:

- Creating *The Right Environment*
- Ensuring *The Right Personnel Fit*
- Executing *The Right Action*

Changing behavior and sustaining high-performance sales levels cannot happen by training or effective coaching alone. A whole solution that is effective and efficient is required to be systematically implemented over time.

Each of the three equation elements—Environment, Fit, and Action—are interdependent. They feed and build on each other as one element supports the success of the other. The Right Environment makes it easier to attract The Right Fit, which in turn makes it easier to produce The Right Action. Only by addressing all of the three components—environment, fit and action—will your organization reach its full performance potential.

CREATING THE RIGHT ENVIRONMENT

A superior working environment that motivates your employees can make the difference between a high-performing organization and one that is mired in mediocrity.

Our research, and more importantly our experience, has identified eight core components that represent the keys to unleashing peak employee productivity: development, compensation, communication, opportunities, support, relationships, input and trust. (See Figure I-1.)

These factors are critical because they create and maintain the company sales culture that nurtures Frontline salespeople, allowing them to develop their skills while offering encouragement and reward for their efforts.

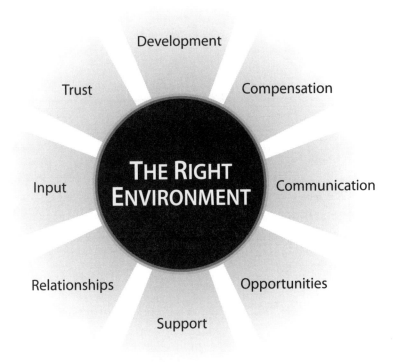

Figure I-1: Eight elements make up The Right Environment portion of the KPE.

This book addresses The Right Environment and how to create it in Chapter 4. There you will also learn how the daily actions of your managers will support the creation of a positive and enabling environment.

The ultimate result is a thriving culture based around taking care of the customer and maximizing sales. This Right Environment then becomes part of the make-up of your company, and simply the way things are done in your organization, effortlessly and seamlessly. It's an incredibly beautiful and rewarding thing!

CREATING THE RIGHT FIT

The fastest way by far to achieve an improvement in sales is by selecting top producers. (See Figure I-2.) Hiring and *keeping* these Right Fit employees becomes much easier if you have The Right Environment. In that situation you will also have to hire less, because turnover is lower. It is also far easier to attract better recruits when your organization provides a productive, positive environment.

THE RIGHT FIT

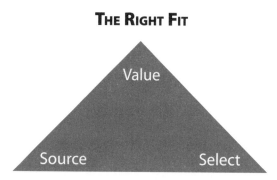

Figure I-2: Value, Source and Select are three key strategies for ensuring The Right Fit in the KPE.

Chapter 5 discusses how to efficiently and effectively source, value and select The Right Fit, and how this reduces turnover, improves morale, and enhances performance.

But don't jump to that chapter right now! The KPE is an interdependent model that needs to be examined in its entirety first.

CREATING THE RIGHT ACTION

The Right Environment and The Right Fit are critical. However, without The Right Action providing clear expectations and continued motivation, they are largely powerless in helping you reach *peak* sales performance. (See Figure I-3.)

In Chapter 6 I will discuss how to identify best-practice sales and service standards and how to effectively measure results. I will also talk about a comprehensive training curriculum that needs to be developed and delivered effectively for results.

Studies, research and, most importantly, our real life experiences, show that people are motivated primarily in three ways: ego (recognition), money (incentive) and fear (accountability). All the training in the world will not get you the desired results if these three factors are not addressed.

THE RIGHT ACTION

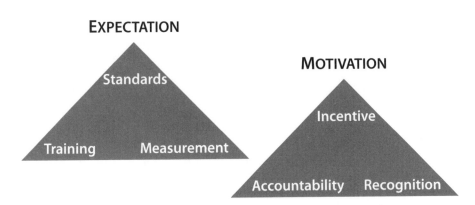

Figure I-3: This section of the KPE is actionable, it is effective and it can get you immediate results as you continue your journey to fully implement the blueprint.

➋ Go "All In" to Win

The best description of culture that I have come across is described as "how things are done around here." For this purpose, I will define "culture" as "how sales are achieved," day in and day out in your organization.

The KPE must be applied in full for a complete transformation to occur. If you decide to pick and choose "cafeteria-style" from this blueprint, depending on your organization, you should expect to get only marginal improvement.

Although some numbers may "pop" for a while, invariably time constraints, focus, turnover, and operational priorities will emerge to derail or frustrate your efforts. They eventually take precedence due to their more "immediate" and "urgent" nature. Before long the "program" will take a back seat to other pressing initiatives, spiraling downward toward mediocrity, far, far from its dramatic profit-vaulting potential.

As we travel together through this book I will discuss sales and sales management strategies and ideas. You will quickly realize that there is a common thread that exists throughout. This familiar thread ties the elements of the KPE that work within a hyper-efficient and impactful performance system.

➋ Make Your Mark and Earn a Place at the Table

> "Lead me, follow me,
> or get out
> of my way."
>
> — George Patton

Joe, my 9-year-old comedian-aspiring son, is constantly (and thankfully, innocently) picking up the latest pop culture phrases. The latest one, "place at the table," has struck a chord with me. A "place at the table" is about earning admiration, respect and making your mark. It is about taking control of your own destiny and taking advantage of great opportunities that you can create or that come your way.

I have experienced three major changes in my career. I sold on the Frontline for three years while in college and just after graduation. To me, averaging $25 an hour in Orlando in 1988 was the best job in town. What was even better was that my base pay was $3.35 per hour, minimum wage at the time!

My second career change came a year out of college, when I became a sales manager in the same industry. I was 25 years old and making $100,000 a year. I did that with an annual base salary that was a whopping $30,000!

My third and final move was to start my own consulting business in 1993 with no salary; zero, zip, not even minimum wage! In the last 15 years we have helped companies make hundreds of millions of dollars in highly profitable revenue. In the process, I have been fortunate enough to generate millions for my firm.

Selling, sales management, sales improvement, and bottom-line results allowed for all those great opportunities. Great things happen to you when you can make *other* people money. In sales, that's what you are able to do.

The sleaze, the tackiness, and the underhanded sales methods of the very few do give selling a bad rap at times. Fortunately, that is the work of a small minority that continues to shrink. The fact is that a career in professional, ethical, above-board selling is both honorable and distinguished.

Selling and this continuing journey have helped me earn my mark, and it has given me incredible opportunities. I know if you embrace it and embrace much of what is in this book, it will, without doubt, do the same for you.

PART 1

TAPPING THE FRONTLINE ADVANTAGE

CHAPTER 1

STARTING WITH THE END IN MIND

"Good business leaders create a vision, articulate the vision, passionately own the vision, and relentlessly drive it to completion."

— Jack Welch

Vision. It is best defined as being able to *visualize* a desired end result—foreseeing exactly where you're going, knowing how you're going to get there, and operating in a way that takes into account the whole of the journey, not just moment-to-moment objectives.

Operating *without* "an end goal in mind" is to work without a purpose, a plan, or direction. But most people simply do not feel it is their role or responsibility to be the visionary for their organization. They believe it is a mantle for someone else to assume.

Vision is only for the super CEO who runs a multibillion dollar enterprise, or for those who have been divinely blessed with the unique talent to see the future and their place in it, right?

Wrong! Establishing a vision is important for everyone. Yes, everyone. It is for the CEO, the entrepreneur, the vice president and other corporate officers, the department, and field managers. It is for you, regardless of your position, or level in your company or organization.

Vision is the mentally crystallized, ultimate goal for your company, your department and the individual roles within it. This goal should address *where* you see yourself, where you see your employees, *how* they handle their customers and the *evolution* of your product.

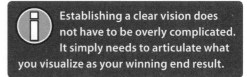

Establishing a clear vision does not have to be overly complicated. It simply needs to articulate what you visualize as your winning end result.

This chapter looks at "the vision thing" and how it relates to supercharging your profits using the Khoury Performance Equation (the KPE).

1

➋ Envision Your Destination and Your Journey

Most of the customers who engage us have one objective in mind: to make more money. While I certainly commend and congratulate those who do call on us, and I most definitely appreciate their business, that expressed objective on its own is just that, an objective—an end point. It does not address much of the strategy or process that will get you there.

The goal of making money, on its own, rarely pans out without understanding that part of that objective needs to include a plan to address two key sets of players in this equation—your team members and your external customers.

Many decision makers who take the time and make the effort to be involved, quickly understand the importance of the KPE blueprint, and before long they begin to own and endorse the process.

However, that type of experience is, unfortunately, not always the case.

Jack "Money Man" Adams

An example of a past client may illustrate this point better.

> "Jack Adams" bought a struggling business with the purpose of "rescuing it," "growing it" and "selling it." Although related to his industry, this was a business in which he had little experience. The mindset that he possessed and believed in revolved mainly around one thing: making money!
>
> Jack had money, wanted more money and money is why he bought this business. Money is how he would attract the best of the best to this business. Money was how he would grow this business, and money was how he would fix this business. Money was the goal, and "without doubt" he was going to make a lot of it.
>
> Jack was the type of owner who only got involved when it was about money. Within two years he had replaced multiple sets of senior managers—people to whom he had paid a great deal of ... you guessed it ... money! Why? They did not make him any money. No one knew the vision or the action plan that was required to reach the business goals. They didn't, because it didn't exist. They were only sure about one thing: they needed to produce more money!
>
> Jack kept hiring manager after manager, paying each one an extremely generous salary—two or three times more than what they had made in

the past, exceeding what the position was worth and what the industry standards dictated. Why? Because in lieu of vision or a real plan, the only thing he knew how to do was to use money to lure in the next "savior" who would then presumably arrive to rescue the business.

The result was that these managers, who were expected to provide miracles, were under a tremendous amount of pressure to make Jack money. Why? Because he was paying them to do so.

Do you think Jack's strategy worked? I don't think I need to tell you, after a lot of *"money"* the business is in bankruptcy.

MAKING MONEY IS NOT A PLAN

Money by itself is neither a vision, nor a system, nor a goal. Money by itself is not a solution. In the case of Jack Adams, where was the vision and the catalyst needed to address the fundamental business issues necessary to make his company a success? How was this company, in an extremely competitive marketplace, going to distinguish itself from the pack and grow?

When I asked Jack about the vision of his business, he said, "The goal right now is to make money." Never was the goal to transform the culture, provide a great environment, or to provide a stable and secure place to work.

In fact, without a clear vision and plan in place, the opposite started to happen:

- Managers at every level got fired and were replaced by higher paid managers. This group put even more of a strain on the P&L, so many of them eventually got fired.

- The focus at the senior level was always on one short-term objective: to make money. The mood this created was that of panic, politics and survival.

- The focus was so much on the amount of money made or lost each day that it clouded the development and nourishment of a real plan to build the business, achieve profit goals and make them stick.

- The panic and the pressure then filtered down to the Frontline, which did produce at some level but certainly nowhere near its potential.

The results, instead, were unhappy employees, unhappy customers, and an awful bottom line.

KHOURY PERFORMANCE STORY

**Happy Employees =
Happy "$1,000/night" Guests**

How do you get a hotel Frontline team, which earns an hourly wage, to provide consistent service levels worthy of a guest experience that can cost $500-$1000 per night? The fundamental answer is rooted in the mantra of Four Seasons founder and CEO Isadore Sharp: "How you treat your employees is how you expect them to treat your customers."

**Here are just
a few things
the Four Seasons
does to create
happy employees:**

- ✔ Outstanding training that lets them enjoy and experience first-class hospitality themselves. Whether employed in housekeeping, the contact center or on the Frontline, a free night's stay with dinner is extended to each team member and a guest.
- ✔ The number of free rooms for employees and their guests continues to increase with tenure.
- ✔ The company contributes 3% to 5% of employees' salary to a 401k and another 3% to 5% to profit sharing.
- ✔ All employees enjoy eating "well" together at the hotel cafeteria.

**The results are
unquestionable:**

- ✔ Average turnover for full-time employees is 18%, half of the industry average.
- ✔ Four Seasons has the distinction to be on *Fortune's* 100 Best Places to Work since 1998. (The survey started in 1998!)
- ✔ A customer base that has something of a "cult-like following."

One customer recently made a compliment to a Four Seasons manager by stating, *"If there is a heaven, it is managed by the Four Seasons."*

Relationships and Results

Regardless of the vision or plan you establish for your company, in the end it is the customer who will ultimately decide whether or not you achieve it, by either buying *your* products and services, or those of your competitor.

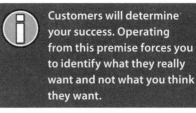

> Customers will determine your success. Operating from this premise forces you to identify what they really want and not what you think they want.

Visualizing the fulfillment of this customer desire through a peak-producing sales team is the first step in creating a Frontline Profit Machine.

No matter what product you sell, your essential areas of influence with your customers can be distilled into two main deliverables:

1. **RELATIONSHIPS:** Map out every customer touch point, whether over the phone, face-to-face, via email, or in other ways. In each interaction, make sure you project the right image, as well as a sincere and enthusiastic desire for their business.

2. **RESULTS:** The real result your customers are looking for is *high value* (whatever they perceive as valuable) for the money they spend with you. Southwest Airlines consistently gets top honors for service levels because the value they offer exceeds the expectations of the customer. That expectation is obviously not the same on all airlines, and becomes significantly higher on a first-class seat on Delta that may be four times the price. Expectation and value: make sure your offering lives up to both.

WE ALL SELL ONLY <u>TWO</u> THINGS

POSITIVE PROFESSIONAL **RELATIONSHIPS**
and
BOTTOM-LINE **RESULTS**

Figure 1-1: Success with customers comes down to relationships and results.

These principles also apply to the interaction that exists between all team members and direct reports in the company: from midlevel managers, to the Frontline managers, to the Frontline salespeople. Delivering these values consistently will provide a win-win-win for your employees, your business, and most importantly, your customers.

➜ Your Most Valuable Asset ... Really

In poll after poll executives are asked what they consider to be their most valuable assets. Invariably, most of them say (you probably guessed it) "our people." The follow-up question on what they do with or how

> ⓘ An organization can run like a robot, but its most vital parts are not robotic; they are imperfect, emotional and often unpredictable human beings.

much they invest in this "most important asset" is often met with very weak and unconvincing answers. Furthermore, if your Frontline people are such great assets, why do so many organizational leaders entrust them and their development to poor, unskilled, and/or unmotivated managers?

Regardless of your business model or your vision for it, at the end of the day it is *people* who execute it. An organization can run like a robot, but its most vital parts are not robotic; they are imperfect, emotional and often unpredictable human beings. Many companies spend millions on business improvement processes but frequently neglect this vital area.

➜ Managers: From Task Masters to Revenue Generators

As you formulate your winning end results, ask yourself this: Are your managers taskmasters, or are they revenue generators? Do *you* really comprehend the difference? Do *they?*

Managers across multiple levels in most organizations are often so saddled with tasks that they miss the opportunity to become revenue-generating leaders. They focus too much on small day-to-day duties and too little on the big mission at hand: generating revenue.

Let's face it: Some tasks are necessary, but many are not. Make sure your managers are not hiding behind these "tasks" to avoid the Frontline. Be aware of how much their "administrative" focus is taking away from your "sales" focus.

Many CEOs do not understand the huge profit impact that Frontline revenue can have when most other expenses are paid for. And the few that do usually do not understand that creating a thriving sales culture requires much more than telling managers to "get sales up," "put a contest together," or to just "focus on it."

Simply having the managers tell the Frontline to ask for "fries with that" just won't cut it.

The same elements of the KPE that get the Frontline salespeople to perform have to be applied to Frontline managers as well. Although it is unrealistic to expect them all to be dynamic, motivational high-powered coaches, it is realistic and necessary to expect that they support and focus on sales and service.

> **i** Few managers know their team's true potential. Many are not comfortable with sales and most do not know how to help their team reach its full potential.

Later chapters discuss how to get all Frontline managers to make sales support a top priority. We will also discuss a sales manager's unique responsibility in more detail.

➋ The Frontline: From Order-Takers to Sales Professionals

Consider these questions. Are your Frontline people order-takers, or are they sales professionals? Do *you* really comprehend the difference? Do *they?*

Were they hired with the understanding that they needed to sell? Do you have the right people? Are they teachable? Are they driven, committed, and motivated?

How do they view their position? Do they understand the powerful impact they have on the profit of your business? Do they understand the great opportunity they have? Do they believe in their products and services and the value they bring to your customer?

The KPE blueprint emphasizes professional ongoing training, effective incentive planning, accountability and support. How many of these critical elements are in place in your organization?

If your people are "fulfilling" orders or, at best, giving it the "ol' college try" every now and then, don't panic; you are part of the vast majority. In fact, I would suggest that you *actually celebrate* because you are a prime candidate for a Frontline Profit Machine and all the benefits and profits that it can bring your organization.

"Feelings, nothing more than feelings ..."

These lyrics may come be from a sappy song, but when it comes to your business, your feelings, your intuition, and what you see and hear, absolutely do count. Over the last 15 years in my business I just know there are things that feel right and there are things that just don't.

As you craft a new vision for your organization, visit your counters, your sales floor, your call-center, and your representatives in the field. Listen and observe how your team interacts with your customers. Take a good, hard look. What are the feelings you get?

How do your Frontline team members view your customers?

- Do they *consistently* view each customer as a valuable gift, or do they view them as just another transaction?

- Do they *consistently* greet customers warmly and enthusiastically?

- Do they *consistently* see the innate good in each customer? Do they empathize, or do they have the feeling that most customers are "cheap," "rude," or view them as a "necessary headache"?

- Do they *consistently* mirror the customers, ask questions, listen for answers, and have a general "do-what-it-takes-to-help-them" attitude?

- Do they *consistently* prioritize their work with the mindset of always meeting and exceeding customer expectations?

- Do they *consistently* believe in your company, in the product they sell, in the value of the price they ask for that product, and in the benefit it gives each and every customer?

- Do they *consistently* represent your business in the best possible light?

- Do they *consistently* act as strong ambassadors for your brand?

 How your company makes your customer feel is the most important and powerful thing you can offer.

→ Meeting Customer Expectations

Meeting expectations is just that: meeting an expectation that a customer has in engaging your services or buying your product. It is transactional; it says "I pay you for something and you deliver it."

Doing a good job of meeting expectations is important and certainly better than not doing so, but it does not move the needle too much for you. Simply meeting minimum expectations is what

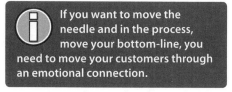

If you want to move the needle and in the process, move your bottom-line, you need to move your customers through an emotional connection.

most companies do; it really is a "yawner" and not very exciting for anybody.

You "move" your customers by the actions of your Frontline. You move your customers by making them "happy." You make them happy by making sure your own *internal customers,* the people who work for you, are "happy" and are in the "mood" to consistently do the best they can with your external customers.

HALF OF YOUR OFFERING

This impact you make on your customers revolves around how you make them "feel" during that short period of interaction. If they feel *better* about you and themselves while they are doing business with you, you have that customer for life.

> It is the emotional mind, or the emotional recollection of how we felt at a particular occasion, that drives our future behavior. As Dr. Joseph LeDoux, a world-renowned neuroscientist at New York University, said in a recent interview: **"Emotions are not designed to be controlled. They are designed to control. In truth, most of what we do, we do unconsciously, and then rationalize the decision consciously after the fact."**

In essence, we make decisions based on emotion and then buttress those decisions with "support thinking." This subtle but incredibly meaningful influence is created through simple actions such as:

- Greeting the guest in your business quickly
- Displaying sincerity and enthusiasm
- Actively listening and understanding

- Being responsive to their needs and doing more "to serve them"
- Appealing to their ego and making them feel important

These are all soft skills that add to the customer's overall positive perception, and woven together, they amount to half of your service! Let me say it again:

> ⓘ **Your Frontline's soft skills and how they make customers feel are at least HALF of your service or product's value!**

"Tasks" vs. "Customers"

Six years ago, Alliant Credit Union faced an extraordinary challenge. The credit union was deeply tied to United Airlines, which in 2002, was facing bankruptcy. Alliant had to leave United or risk insolvency in the competitive and unforgiving world of banking. It had to figure out quickly how to find new revenue sources. Sound familiar?

"We were not a low-performing organization trying to turn around. For decades, we were efficient, profitable. We enjoyed very high client satisfaction," says Lee Schafer, senior vice president of corporate affairs. *"But we were facing a stark and fundamental challenge. In the past, we could ride out poor revenue cycles with our parent company, but those days are history. We had to make some changes. We realized what had worked before wouldn't work anymore. What we wanted to achieve—more customers, revenue and profit, depended on having a new breed of managers."*

"We came from a management culture that was very task oriented; management was really just supervising people performing tasks," says Alliant CEO David W. Mooney, who arrived in 2003. *"Managers had very little responsibility beyond organizing and monitoring tasks, and their development responsibilities were largely limited. We [needed] to change that ethic to create true managers responsible for performance management and development."*

When Alliant first measured their team connectedness, only 21% of their workforce said they were "engaged." By 2006 that number had grown to 63%. Did it work? You be the judge. Credit Union membership vaulted by 23% from 168,643 to over 200,000 members in three years and loan values skyrocketed from just under $1.75 billion to over $2.3 billion, an increase of over 31% … all this happened in the context of losing their primary source of business!

The emotional connection that your customers experience, and the feelings they get from your business, have nothing to do with managers filling out mundane reports to send to the corporate office. Your customers are not emotionally moved by your managers attending the third cost-cutting meeting of the month, or the fourth conference call on the latest new product strategy.

Of course, all managers have to meet the operational requirements necessary to make your business run. However, the priority must always be on meeting the immediate needs of *their customers*—their internal ones (the Frontline staff) so they can deliver to your external customers (paying patrons) what they are looking for.

The End Result: Critical Elements and Components

In the end, your particular vision or goal can materialize only if it is built around *relationships* and *results, developed both internally and externally.*

When visualizing your successful end result, consider these questions:

- Where do you want your company to go?
- What type of revenue and profit do you want to generate?
- What image do you want the Frontline to project for you in the marketplace?
- What type of team and company culture do you want to establish?
- What personal impact do you want to have on your team and your company?
- What do you want to be remembered for?

Although I cannot define your specific vision, I can speculate based on some of the most common things which many of us in the sales and business arena are striving for:

Happy employees, elated customers, and impressively growing profits are a great start. Add in more personal free time, better work/life balance, less stress, and for an owner, a higher business valuation, and you have something really worth pursuing.

◢ Steps to Success

This is what many business books dub "the moment of truth." The salesperson-customer interaction is what really matters. Everything you do—operations, merchandising, and marketing—is about creating this moment.

Ask yourself and your team: Is there anything more important? Take your time to really absorb that question. This is about how your Frontline handles your customer, how they service them, how they sell them and how they make them feel. Is there anything more critical in your business? What do you think, what do you believe and more importantly, what do you demonstrate?

Start with the end in mind. Figure 1-2 illustrates how to best depict this to your team.

Figure 1-2: Working through these steps will help you define and execute your ultimate goal.

THE IDEAL INTERACTION

This is about the professional and positive service you would like your team to provide, which is equally as important as the sale you would like them to make. How do you envision a *great* sale? What should professional service-based selling, cross-selling and up-selling scenarios look like in your organization? How should they *"feel"* to your customer?

THE REVENUE GOAL

Do you believe that you can influence the performance of your salespeople, or do you feel they are just "born that way" and that you are simply lucky to have a "few really good ones"?

Do you believe that most employees just cannot or do not want to perform at a top level? Do you believe you can duplicate the efforts of your "really good ones"? What about improving the performance of your top producers? Is it even possible? I am here to tell you that the answer to all of these questions is a resounding and an absolute *yes!*

Your specific sales goal will, of course, depend on your business.

Imagine this: What if your location produced what the average of your top 10% or even the top 20% salespeople are producing in up-sell, cross-sell and/or conversion revenue?

If you are like most companies we have worked for, *I would venture to say that the number will be at least 30% better than what your company is doing today.* If this is true in your business, which is highly likely, your minimum goal is set!

IMPACT ON YOUR CUSTOMER

Here are a few beliefs on customer impact that I would hope you will buy into. (See Figure 1-3):

THE KHOURY GUIDING PRINCIPLES

Figure 1-3: The Khoury Key Tenets of Service-Based Sales

Without doubt, your customers will be happier if you do these things. Subscribing to these principles is the first step to making them all happen!

If you believe in these tenets, and you couple this conviction with a proven formula for success and then galvanize them with a strong commitment to achieve these goals, then you are on your way. You are now in much more control of the well-being of your customers—all of them—which in turn will result in the well-being of your balance sheet.

IMPACT ON YOUR TEAM

Now it is time to ask these questions when it comes to the impact on your team:

- How does creating a positive and trusting sales environment impact your team?
- Does training, communicating, involving and supporting your team improve morale and lower turnover?
- How will the fact that you can now justify paying your team members more money out of the new found revenue they help produce impact them and their families?
- Are your managers happier with a plan that gives them the tools to positively impact their employees which, in the process, build both your and their bottom line?

Do you, without question, believe your team will be happier if this all happens? If the answer is yes, don't just thumb through this book, immerse yourself in its message.

IMPACT ON YOUR BUSINESS

Many managers and owners come from an accounting background. As such they are very conscience of the cost side of the operation. Managing your business through a Profit & Loss statement is certainly a smart thing to do but doing so alone can be crippling. It takes money to make money, and it takes an investment in people for them to sell and produce. If all the KPE is in place, that investment can be the single best thing you spend money on in your business.

You need to know what a 20% or 30% conversion means to your revenue and your bottom line? How does a 20% up-sell conversion on a value-added product or service impact your revenue and profit?

Once you have addressed the fundamentals in your business—a sound business model, a great product, an effective marketing plan, a well-run operation—is there anything you can think of that is more important than selling at the Frontline?

Is there anything more important and satisfying than having happy customers, happy employees and a great bottom line? If you truly *believe*—a word I will repeat over and over again—congratulations! You have addressed the first critical part of what is needed to achieve a very prosperous and successful organization.

The Name of the Game is Transformation

Transforming a business culture into a committed, service-based sales environment starts with creating happy, productive employees. They, in turn, provide better service that better satisfies your customers. These customers then spend more money with you and drive your profits upward, which gives you more freedom to support your team. The influences are all circular and interdependent. Sound easy enough?

Achieving this culture change requires defining roles, systemizing procedures, establishing clear expectations, and then putting a motivational plan in place to accelerate execution. This leverages your capabilities by allowing others to perform crucial culture-building tasks that you are unable or do not have time to perform yourself.

It allows you to manage from a higher altitude, and enjoy your work experience while granting you more free time. And you deserve it! What good is achievement if it costs you everything else to acquire it?

Generating revenue through happy, motivated Frontline representatives who are energized and creative can produce a nearly autonomous way to springboard profits. This greater cash production also builds the intrinsic value and marketability of your enterprise.

> *A study done by Gallup on publicly traded companies with varying levels of "employee engagement" revealed that organizations that ranked in the top 25% in worker job satisfaction generated 2.6 times more in earnings per share than companies that were below average.*
>
> *Also consider this study by Alex Edmans, a finance professor at University of Pennsylvania's Wharton School. His finding reveals that companies in Fortune's list of 100 best companies to work for had stock prices that rose 14% per year from 1998 to 2005, as compared to a 6% rise for the market overall. Incredible stock numbers, happy employees, and happy customers—I think you would agree that this makes a good foundation for a people-centered Frontline Profit Machine.*

> "Things may come to those who wait, but only the things left over by those who hustle."
>
> — Abraham Lincoln

This vision is *unattainable* only if you do not a have clear idea of what it is you are attempting to accomplish or lack a roadmap to bring you there.

The bottom line is this: If you believe in your vision and you really want to achieve it, the best time to step up and take a leadership role in making it happen is *now*.

Is it easy? Not one bit! *Fortune estimates that about 70% of companies can't execute on strategy and that only 10% of organizations actually attain their strategic objective.*

Can you do it? Only if you are open minded, persistent, diligent, ready to acknowledge past mistakes and shortcomings, and admit you need help!

Is it worth it? You tell me! If the answer is "Yes!" then let's get started!

KHOURY KEY TAKEAWAYS

CHAPTER 1

Create a vision and clarify your **winning end result.**

Understand and appreciate that achieving this vision is a plan that includes:

- ✔ *Happy employees* that translates to *happy customers* who then enable a great *bottom line.*
- ✔ What customers really want:
  - Positive professional relationships
  - Bottom-line results

NO-BULL KNOW HOW!

1. Define the best practice customer interaction.

2. Define the revenue goal. *Most Frontline organizations have a 20% to 50% improvement potential.*

3. Understand, appreciate and sell the positive win-win outcome as a result of:

- ✔ Impact on customer
- ✔ Impact on team
- ✔ Impact on company bottom line

4. Communicate the commitment to a culture transformation through:

- ✔ The *Khoury Performance Equation* as the blueprint to achieve your winning end-result.

BANKING ON IT!

Meeting operational requirements is critical. *"Operations"* execution alone however, is overrated! Today's businesses need a *Frontline Profit Machine*

- ✔ Pick up on the feelings at your Frontline and understand the mindset of your team.

- ✔ Make your customer feel great; moving your customers emotionally moves your bottom line positively.

- ✔ Move managers from taskmasters to revenue generators.

- ✔ Move Frontline from order-takers to professional salespeople.

- ✔ You have to commit and go *all in to win.*

CHAPTER 2

MAKING THE CASE FOR A *FRONTLINE* PROFIT MACHINE

"One of the great mistakes is to judge policies and programs by their intentions rather than their results."

— *Milton Friedman*

Understanding the theory behind creating a Frontline Profit Machine is all well and good, and I hope you have bought into the general concept and value of doing so. But that's not enough? You're a smart businessperson, and I wouldn't expect you to commit to this blueprint before looking carefully at the supporting data.

You may already be asking these questions:

- Does this stuff apply to my organization?
- How much money are we currently leaving on the table?

Straightforward questions usually require straightforward answers: You need to look at each of your customer "contact points" and figure out what influence your Frontline can have through them.

There is also one more challenge, which is selling this plan to your employees and senior decision makers. You have to make the case and then back it up with numbers. The purpose of this chapter is to provide you with extensive case studies and a bottom-line rationale for implementing the Khoury Performance Equation (the KPE).

➋ Customer Contact Points

"Flavor" is not the main reason that customers return to fast-food chains. According to Gallup research, the quality of the interactions customers have

with the people who take their orders and serve them is what is most important. In general, diners who feel that the staff stands out are roughly five times more likely to return.

If you map out all of your customer contact points, you will find that many of them present substantial revenue opportunities, and all of them provide significant service-improvement opportunities.

> **"Customers are not looking for transactions; they're looking for relationships. People can transact their business pretty much anywhere they want."**
>
> — John Fleming,
> author of Human Sigma

Here are a few examples:

HOTEL: *Seven customer contact points and potential sales opportunities*

- Contact center: Booking reservations, room upgrades, excursions, spa services
- Internet via email interaction, click-to-chat and proactive chat: Booking reservations, room upgrades, excursions, spa services
- Front Desk: Selling additional amenities, i.e., room upgrades, view upgrades, dry cleaning, in-house restaurant reservations, excursions and spa services
- Room Service: Upgrading average ticket
- Restaurant: Upgrading average ticket
- Gift Shop: Selling higher margin items
- Concierge: Limo transfers, excursions

HOME IMPROVEMENT STORE: *Five customer touch points and potential sales opportunities*

- Phone Receptionist: Projecting professionalism and a high degree of knowledge to draw the customers into the store
- Phone Salespeople: Selling products and services to draw customers into the store for further obligation
- Floor Salespeople: Selling products, product packages, cross-sells and up-sells
- Installers: Selling warranties, such as "scotch guard" for carpeting; additional products, services, such as baseboards for flooring; increasing the scope of job
- Cashier: Selling high-margin products in the checkout aisle, pointing out ancillary and complimentary products

Some of these touch points have huge potential; others may not. I may have also missed one or two since many similar businesses may offer other unique opportunities. But think about the impact a superstar service-oriented salesperson could have in these positions versus that of your average or poor performer. It can be explosive.

➋ Sales Opportunities

The most substantial new revenue opportunities exist through either indirect or direct sales interactions. In fact, in many cases one leads to the other.

INDIRECT SALES OPPORTUNITIES

Indirect sales opportunities are ones that tend to be the most overlooked in many organizations. The positions that offer them are often viewed as entry-level, with little thought as to the profit influence they have. Further, because they are generally low-paying positions drawing on mostly younger, less-educated and "less experienced" people, the confidence level in these representatives to positively influence customers is also very low.

However, these positions are critical to an organizations success. Tapping into this potential revenue reservoir will give you a competitive edge since it's something few companies employ and even fewer companies employ *well*. Here are a few examples:

- **Bank Teller:** A bank teller is able to build rapport, look at a customer's balance, recognize a customer need, and then recommend and set up an appointment with a sales specialist.

- **Receptionist (any industry):** A receptionist may handle a customer inquiry that can be as simple as directions to the store or dealership. He or she influences the customers' perception of the company and whether they actually visit the store and eventually make a purchase.

- **Insurance Agency Customer Service Personnel:** A professional service agent handling a service or complaint call on a customer's homeowner's policy can build rapport and, after resolving the issue, confidently "warm transfer" the customer to the auto specialist in the agency for a quote on car insurance.

- **Contact Center Service Salesperson (any industry):** Any request for service can lead to uncovering a multitude of needs and subsequent chances for an "upgrade," a "new solution," or an "updated" product or service. This salesperson can then set up the opportunity for the sales specialist, who can then close the sale. In an ideal case scenario, this can be done immediately while the customer is still on the phone.

These are often-overlooked-but-vital members of sales organizations. They have the ability to capitalize on the subtle, but powerful opportunities that can provide a critical competitive edge to your business.

BY THE NUMBERS

Look at these examples and see if you can apply them to your organization:

A bank teller helps 500 customers a week. What is the profit impact if that teller converts five (or five more) customers a week to an appointment for a financial specialist or loan officer, even if the loan officer closes just one out of those five referrals?

Assume the profit (which in reality is exponential, as there are very little added marketing or infrastructure costs) is $500 per year for each conversion.

Let's do the math:

- 500 bank customers per week
- 5 new referrals
- 1 sale for $500/profit
- $500/week = $25,000 per year per teller of additional referred profit ($500 * 50 weeks)
- 5 tellers in the branch mean additional profit of $125,000.
- 20 banks in the region then means $2.5 million.
- 82 banks in the state means … it gets scary!

Now apply that same logic to your receptionists, who can easily influence five more customers that come into your dealership or your place of business.

Or how about your contact center salesperson, who handles 100 service calls a day? What will transferring five more customers to a sales specialist for an "upgrade" or a "cross sell" mean to your profit if as little as one of those customers actually purchases something?

Direct Sales Opportunities

Direct sales opportunities are even more powerful. When those on the Frontline are able to sell to customers effectively, the possibilities are staggering.

Here are a few of the positions that are often overlooked or undervalued in their tremendous profit-building potential:

- » Contact Center Salesperson
- » Restaurant Server
- » Loan Officer
- » Financial Advisor
- » Retail Salesperson
- » Insurance Agent
- » Coffee Barista
- » Real Estate Agent
- » Convenience Store Clerk
- » Rent-a-Car Agent
- » Rent-an-Anything Salesperson
- » Car Care Service Advisor
- » Dealership Service Advisor
- » Auto Salesperson
- » Movie Theater Concession Attendant
- » Any Concession Stand Attendant
- » Fast Food Order Taker
- » Pharmaceutical Sales Rep
- » Outside Sales Rep
- » Postal Service Rep
- » Apartment Leasing Agent

> **i** Many common businesses can actually double their profits by improving their top-line revenue by just 5% to 10%.

But don't just take my word for it. Read on!

Defining Profit Potential

Defining upside potential is central to your journey in the Khoury Performance Equation. Nothing is more difficult to sell than an abstract, subjective, and invisible outcome. Therefore, you have to become skilled, not just at talking about this potential, but at clearly quantifying it as well.

UPSIDE POTENTIAL: A SIMPLE EXERCISE

Defining your upside potential emphasizes your possible end result. This justifies your effort, your time, and the investment required to make the improvements a reality.

I touched on this in the introduction, but it is important to reiterate and it is critical for you to fully take in this simple yet powerful reality. The simplest way to determine upside sales potential in your business is to perform this simple exercise:

Look at the production of your average salesperson, and then compare it to your top-10% producers. You will see that in many cases, even in situations where the sales opportunity is relatively equal between employees, the disparity in their sales production is 30% to 60% or higher. *This tells you that an improvement of at least 30% is entirely possible!*

This is not a difficult conclusion to buttress or sell as an opportunity because both levels are already being achieved! The potential becomes even more profound and realistic when you consider many of your "top performers," those who are in the "top 10%," can also improve.

PEAK POTENTIAL, NOT PERCEIVED POTENTIAL

A key principle in the message from this book is to go for your full potential not just for improvement.

Compare overall performance to your peak top performers. Now imagine the behavior of your high flyers becoming the new norm in your organization. If you have found a few people who can perform at this level, *why not duplicate them across your entire Frontline team instead of accepting mediocre or poor performance from the other 90%?*

Take a look at the tremendous impact each individual team member has on your revenue and profit. Many of our clients are experts when it comes to their P&L statement. However, when it comes to the revenue and profit potential that *just one of* their Frontline representatives influences

> **i** Aspire toward your "peak" potential, not your "perceived" potential, which is artificially bound by the people and the processes in place now.

each year, the most common response we encounter is: "Geez! I just didn't realize that."

> **i** This money is being "left on the table" when it could be right on your bottom line!

Changing the Paradigm: A Bottom-line View

Now look at that peak potential concept further with examples from a few different industries. Ask yourself these questions:

- How do I view my Frontline?

- How do my *managers* view our Frontline?

- How do our *customers* view our Frontline?

> "To exist is to change, to change is to mature, to mature is to go on creating oneself endlessly."
>
> — Henri Bergson, French Nobel Prize winning philosopher

Then, consider some of these industry-specific questions:

- Is your salesperson on the phone selling a home movie channel for $10 a month or is he or she representing three years of hassle-free, convenient entertainment for $360? **It's all in the language.**

- Is your full-service car wash service advisor upgrading a ticket by $4, or is he or she adding 20% to your annual revenue (80% of which directly hits your bottom line)? **It's all in your perspective.**

- Are the sales warranty services at your electronics store a nicety, offered begrudgingly and robotically by your floor personnel, or are they shared as valuable peace-of-mind products? Are your team members aware in many cases that this sale represents almost all of your transaction profit? **It's all in the value you place.**

- Is your leasing agent "pressuring" a potential renter into a lease or is that person writing up a $10,000 per year agreement and inviting a prospective valuable resident into your community for many years to come? **It's all in the belief you have.**

"Dollarize" it. Put the numbers to it and annualize your Frontline team members' impact. Then ask yourself, "Is there a better intiative I can execute to achieve this level of added profit contribution with less capital risk?"

If you are like most businesses that interface directly with the consumer, *90% of your revenue flows through your Frontline employees.* Understanding and valuing that impact is a critical first step in your mission of developing a Frontline Profit Machine.

➋ KPE in the Real World: Seven Case Studies

Following are some real-world examples that demonstrate the dynamic effect of the KPE on Frontline-generated profit. They represent what are considered by many to be "tough" industries, those with traditionally high employee turnover and/or low profit margins.

Choose the one that best aligns with your business. Although I urge you to study all seven, there are lessons to be learned from each.

Case Study #1: The Contact Center

case study

Consider this:

- The contact center industry is one of the largest employers in North America.
- It is also booming in emerging economies around the world.
- For the most part, contact center performance is measured in terms of cost, *not in terms of improved revenue.*

Measuring revenue growth in this industry can be very challenging, especially when it comes to clearly determining the actual catalysts for improvement. This challenge surfaces consistently because when numbers improve, questions invariably arise.

Did sales improve because:

- Your competition raised prices?
- You lowered prices?
- Your competition is having challenges?
- Your marketing department spent more on advertising or because they came up with a brilliant campaign?

It's often very difficult to put your finger on the answers. As a result, contact center managers frequently find themselves in a no-win situation: They get very little credit when the numbers go up, but they are blamed or are conveniently made "scapegoats" when numbers are stagnant or go down.

Answer the challenge:

Apply the logic of sales production differential as described as the gap (in performance) between your top, average, and bottom producers who have similar sales opportunities. This, along with a full deployment of the KPE, will produce results that are substantial enough to dismiss any meaningful credit commonly attributed elsewhere for smaller sales increases.

No single actionable initiative can produce more for your organization than the crafting of a high-performance service-based sales culture. When you calculate the impact of a motivated producer in a contact center (following the KPE), you will find that the numbers can be mind-blowing.

Example: Package Travel Tour Company Operating Own Charter

- Type: Annual inbound contact center
- Volume: $50 million
- Bottom-line profit: 10% ($5 million)
- Number of salespeople: 50
- Pre-KPE annual revenue per salesperson: $1 million
- Pre-KPE average revenue per booking: $4,000
- Average annual days worked per salesperson per year: 250
- Pre-KPE Bookings per salesperson per day: 1

Forecasted Impact after Full Implementation of the KPE

- The top 10% of salespeople book $1.8 million per year (80% above average)
- One more booking per day per salesperson doubles revenue
- Realistic potential is 50% improvement or $25 million per year (destination capacity permitting)

 Estimated bottom-line impact: $7.5 million per year, all without adding one additional inbound call!

Winning End Results

- ✔ **150% improvement in bottom line! ($7.5 million/$5.0 million = +150%)**
- ✔ Happier Employees ... due to better income!
- ✔ Happier Customers ... due to better needs/wants assessment and fulfillment!
- ✔ Happier Management ... due to greater security, lower turnover and lower stress!
- ✔ Happier Stockholders ... due to higher profits and ROI!

Case Study #2: The Full-Service Car Wash

case study

Consider this:

The full-service car wash industry is highly fragmented and can be extremely challenging as variables that influence success are highly volatile and extreme.

For investors, the barrier to entry is relatively low. You find many financiers justifying their purchase because of the real estate ownership involved. They may also view the business itself as an easy opportunity that can be simply outsourced to a manager.

Labor is the single biggest line item frequently accounting for 50% of total expenses. Controlling that cost is crucial. When it rains you have no choice but to send people home, which helps payroll but severely increases turnover. In fact, due to a variety of factors, annual turnover commonly exceeds 150%, even in superbly run businesses.

Having said that, operators who do know what they are doing can be very successful. A sharp single-site operator can pay his debt down over six or seven years and begin netting high six figures regularly.

Answer the challenge:

Understanding how to buy and maintain equipment, how to implement basic marketing strategies and run the operation efficiently is paramount. Once that is mastered, the real profit comes down to servicing customers professionally and raising the average revenue per ticket by offering higher-end washes, details and other additional services.

Improving revenues at the point of sale can easily double profits, as the following real-world example illustrates.

Example: Full-service Car Wash with Detail Bays

- Annual number of washes performed: 80,000
- Average pre-KPE revenue per wash: $17.00
- Pre-KPE revenue per year: $1.36 million
- Pre-KPE annual profit: 15% or $204,000

Forecasted Impact After Full Implementation of KPE

- Upgrade 10% of customers to details for an additional $20.00 per ticket = $160,000
- Upgrade 20% of customers to superior wash packages for an additional $10.00 per ticket = $160,000
- Combined revenue improvement is an additional $320,000 per year or $4 per ticket

 Estimated bottom-line impact: 75% of $320,000 or $240,000 per year, all without adding one additional customer!

Winning End Results

- ✔ **117% improvement on bottom line! ($240,000/$204,000 = +117 %)**
- ✔ Happier employees
- ✔ Happier customers
- ✔ Happier owners

 **Case Study #3: The Retail Sales Store**

case study

Consider this:

Retail is tough, especially if you are relying on inexperienced labor whose main motivation for taking a part-time job at the mall is "to make some money *and* to socialize." And not necessarily in that order!

Answer the challenge:

Forget about industry standards on what your sales staff should be paid. Measure their impact, put a number to it and look at ROI when it comes to how you pay them. If you have the right pay plan, the people that you pay the most to should be by far your "best value." That is, the more you pay them, the more you are able to keep for yourself.

If your incentive plan pays well, you will attract better candidates who will stick around longer and give you more. Then, before you know it, the word spreads around the "mall" and the better salespeople want to work for you!

Combine a strong team with a good product, great training, continuous coaching and service and sales-oriented managers, and you will shatter the traditional metrics that exist in retail.

Here's a real-world example of this transformational impact:

Example: Casual Clothing Store at Local Mall

- Annual store visitors: 300,000
- Annual pre-KPE average ticket: $50
- Pre-KPE conversion: 15% or 45,000 annual tickets
- Pre-KPE revenue: $2.25 million
- Pre-KPE margin: 25%
- Opportunity:
    » Increase conversion 7 points to 22% for a new total of 66,000 tickets per year.
    » Top performers have a ticket average of $75. Use a conservative estimate of $60 per ticket for overall new average performance.

Forecasted Impact After Full Implementation of the KPE

- Annual store visitors: 300,000
- Revised average ticket: $60.00
- New conversion: 22% or 66,000 annual tickets
- Revised revenue: $3.96 million
- Revised margin: 32%
- Revised profit: $1.287 million

 Estimated bottom-line improvement: $724,500 per year, all without advertising for one additional customer!

Winning End Results

- ✓ **144% improvement on bottom line! ($724,500/$562,500 = +144%)**
- ✓ Happier employees
- ✓ Happier customers
- ✓ Happier general manager
- ✓ Happier owner

case study   ## Case Study #4: The Car Rental Industry

Consider this:

Car rental is a very tough industry with notoriously low margins. A 2008 Chevy Malibu is the same product, whether you rent it from Avis or Jack's Rents for Less.

Price is the competitive edge for many car rental companies. In many cases, it is the only way for them to gain a customer. For many operators, what and how much they sell on the counter determines if they make money, lose money or close their doors.

Answer the challenge:

In many cases, an increase of 5% to 7% in top-line revenue will at least *double* the net operating profit. The ability to do this is not inhibited at all by competitors' whims or by what the economy does. Rather, it falls back on what you do with your staff and your own service and sales program.

Doubling profits in this manner is totally within reach, as the following real-world case study depicts:

Example: Airport and Local Market Operator

- Number of fleet cars: 2,500
- Pre-KPE utilization: 80%
- Pre-KPE rental days sold per year: 730,000
- Pre-KPE average daily rate: $35.00
- Pre-KPE average incremental per day Revenue: $6
- Pre-KPE total average daily rate: $41
- Pre-KPE revenue per year: $29,930,000
- Pre-KPE annual profit: 6% or $1,795,800

Forecasted Impact After the Full Implementation the KPE

- Upgrade 12% of customers into more comfortable vehicles at an average increase of $15 per day (12% x $15.00 = $1.80 increase per rental day).

- Sell 7% more of added *"peace-of-mind"* coverages and damage responsibility waiver products at an average increase of $18.00 per day (7% x $18.00 = $1.26 increase per rental day).

- New daily rate: $41.00 + $1.80 + $1.26 = $44.06

- Increased incremental revenue: ($1.80 + $1.26) x 730,000 days per year = $2,233,800

- Increase utilization by 3 points through increased local market phone bookings and airport walk-ups.

- 2500 cars x 3% x 365 days per year = 27,375 added rental days x $44.06 = $1,206,142

- Potential revenue increase: $2,233,800 + $1,206,142 = $3,439,942

Estimated bottom-line impact: (65% * $3,439,942 = +$2,235,962)

Winning End Results

- ✓ **124% improvement on bottom line! ($2,235,962/$1,795,800 = 124.5%)**
- ✓ Happier employees
- ✓ Happier customers
- ✓ Happier owner, executives and managers
- ✓ Happier stockholders

Case Study #5: The Apartment Home Community

case study

Consider this:

The margins in this industry are striking once you start reaching the higher occupancy levels. The real-estate cost is the same home community, whether you have 78% or 93% tenancy. Moreover, you also enjoy other economies-of-scale with fixed costs for things like local and headquarters administration, common area maintenance, property taxes and so forth.

As you can see, it is these few percentage points in occupancy that produce the *highly profitable revenue* that can mean the difference between printing your P&L in black or printing it in red. A few more percentage points could mean the difference between an average year and a spectacular year. And a spectacular year could make you, the regional manager, district manager or apartment complex manager a hero—or a genius. Whichever you prefer.

So how do you get there? First, you need to realize the value housed in your front office and in the Frontline employees who answer the phone and showcase the property. Yes, having people who are "administratively capable" is important, but that is not enough. What really counts is assembling team members who can command the interest of that customer on the phone and then close the sale when they come in to see the property.

Answer the challenge:

The secret to success here boils down to an understanding that the true value of that Frontline person is *not* that they can take an order to "rent" an apartment. The real value is in their ability to close the sale on an apartment home for $9,600/year with the prospect of renewing it for many years to come.

That's a big deal! Success comes with the knowledge that your people can build rapport over the phone, intrigue the customers, capture their imagination, invite them to visit the property, and then emotionally tether them to it when they visit.

And by the way … forget about the new complex down the road that has grand opening specials! You can't control that. Build up the belief in your people about your property, its benefits and its value. *People buy from people, and people buy into people.* Your customers want nice neighbors, and your Frontline staff can be their first great neighbor. Understand that concept, plug your numbers into it, and watch your profits go through the roof. Here we go:

Example: Local Apartment Complex

- **Number of units available 800**
- **Pre-KPE occupancy: 78%**
- **Pre-KPE average lease: $9,600 (12 months at $800 per month)**
- **Pre-KPE annual revenue: $5,990,400**
- **Pre-KPE annual margin: 15%**
- **Pre-KPE annual net profit: $898,560**

Forecasted Impact After Full Implementation of the KPE

- Number of units available: 800
- Revised occupancy: 93%
- Average lease: $9,600 (12 months at $800 per month)
- Revised annual revenue: $7,142,400
- Revised annual margin: 25%
- Revised annual net profit: $1,785,600

Winning End Results

✓ **98.7% improvement in bottom line! ($1,785,600/$898,560 = 98.7%)**

✓ **Happier employees**

✓ **Happier residents**

✓ **Happier general manager, executives**

✓ **Happier owners and stockholders**

Case Study #6: The Restaurant Server

case study

Consider this:

The restaurant business! It's famously challenging, unforgiving, competitive and risky. Just ask a bank loan officer! But the KPE can do magic here.

Here is my personal opinion. If your food is just okay but your service is exceptional, I will probably give you another shot. But if your food is great and your service is poor, I am done for good. And guess what? I am in the majority! Unless you fix the problem quickly, I won't be the only one who is "done."

In a very competitive industry it is easy to see that the real margins, again come from the really good stuff—in this case, drinks, appetizers and desserts. Service and sales are truly codependent in this business. You simply cannot strong-arm a customer into your special of the day or a glass of Pinot Grigio. So, why not kill two birds with one stone by improving your service while simultaneously increasing your sales?

Answer the challenge:

Start by discerning the impact of a professional server on your restaurant, regardless of what type of establishment you have.

Incremental products (desserts/specials/drinks) have very high margins (as much as 70%). As in the other cases, most of the fixed costs are paid for (hourly wages, building and insurance costs, etc.). Once you have a vision of what is newly possible, move aggressively to achieve it through the progressive implementation of the KPE.

Here's a real-world example that breaks down this process at a restaurant:

Example: Local Sports-Themed Bar and Restaurant

- Number of people waiter/waitress served per day: 70
- Pre-KPE average revenue per customer: $18.00 ($4.00 from *"extra"* sales)
- Pre-KPE annual revenue per server: $315,000
- Pre-KPE profit margin: 15%
- Pre-KPE annual net margin per server: $47,250
- Pre-KPE annual net margin multiplied by 10 servers: $472,500

Forecasted Impact After Full Implementation of the KPE

- Number of people waiter/waitress served per day: 70
- Revised average revenue per customer: $22.00 ($8.00 now from *"extra"* sales)
- Revised annual revenue per server: $385,000
- Revised profit margin: 25%
- Revised annual net margin per server: $96,250
- Revised annual net margin multiplied by 10 servers = Profit of $962,500

Winning End Results

- ✓ **104% improvement in bottom line! ($490,000/$472,500 = +104%)**
- ✓ **Happier employees**
- ✓ **Happier managers**
- ✓ **Happier customers**
- ✓ **Happier regional manager and executives**
- ✓ **Happier owners and stockholders**

KHOURY PERFORMANCE STORY

From Zero to $23 Million

One of my first clients, Steve Gross, bought the Thrifty Car Rental at Los Angeles Airport franchise for close to nothing. Then, again, when an operation loses money for years it really is not worth a whole lot.

Steve knew car rental like the back of his hand. He knew how to buy cars, how to run an operation, and how to manage costs. Steve also knew that at a base rate of $25 per day and an incremental sales average of $5 per day (the sales of upgrades, coverages etc.) the $30 per day he was getting on average was far short of getting him into the black.

An extra $3 per day per rental would help him break even, an extra $5 per day more would make him good money and $8 per day would make him rich.

Therefore, creating a sales culture at the front counter was not an option; it was a necessity! This was a performance emergency and we had to move fast.

We helped Steve adopt these five key strategies:

1. Design a generous performance-based commission plan
2. Heavy focus on the numbers
3. Recognize top-producing salespeople and managers
4. Train and coach effectively
5. Hold the staff accountable for results

We then moved to recruiting superstars, which was made easier because the pay plan was by far the best in town for those that could produce. We then continued to work on creating a supportive service-based sales environment.

Within six months a new team was in place and we continued to "sculpt and refine" it as more of the KPE elements where introduced. The results were a game-changing $9.50 per day incremental revenue increase, resulting in an extra $250,000 each month in what was now very highly profitable revenue.

Does a Frontline Profit Machine work? Maybe this will answer the question: Twenty years earlier Steve began his career as an hourly rental agent for National Car Rental. Today he is retired after accepting an offer for $23 million for his franchise, and enjoying life with his young family at his beach home in Malibu, California.

Case Study #7: Insurance Office: Combining Direct and Indirect Sales Opportunities

Consider this:

With one of the strongest negative stigmas and stereotypes to overcome in the consumer marketplace, insurance people have their work cut out for them. In this industry, the mindset of "price" is firmly engrained in the Frontline, often permeating into management and ownership levels.

It is almost systemic—leading to a culture that believes cost is the *only* real driver for customers, and that agents don't really *have* that much influence. You have no doubt heard the saying: "The customer knows what he wants." Well, that phrase may have been invented in this industry!

Answer the challenge:

In the real world, the insurance sales dynamic and its potential for improved revenue is a little more complex because opportunities to increase it are available through both direct and indirect means.

Let's dig a bit further into this with another case study. This one features a local client of ours whose Frontline salespersons have generated sizeable opportunities and then made the most of them.

BUSINESS OVERVIEW

- **Description:** Insurance agency specializing in homeowners' policies and auto policies representing over 20 insurance companies.

- **Opportunity:** Increase auto policies by converting more of the 40,000 customers that are current home policy owners to home *and auto* policy owners. Agents interact with customers during inbound service calls about their home policies.

- **Unique Selling Proposition:** Improve service by providing "one-stop shopping" convenience and a high-touch service offering. Offer better rates by promoting alternative A+ insurance companies that don't spend a huge percentage of their budget on advertising.

- **Primary Strategy:** Train and motivate the five service agents who each handle an average of 300 service calls a day, to improve their current conversion of auto quotes to customers from 3% to 30%. Subsequently, get the auto specialist to improve on their closing conversion on the above referrals to realize this tenfold sales opportunity.

- **Implementation:**
  - » Implementing every aspect of the KPE, starting with a gap analysis
  - » Getting buy-in from management on the opportunity that exists
  - » Customizing training, reporting and implementing a new incentive plan. We helped hire the right people, address low performers, eventually separating the wrong people and installing a new dynamic sales management strategy.
  - » Transforming the role of managers and supervisors from task masters to revenue generators
  - » Transforming the role of agents from order takers to sales professionals

Example: Regional Insurance Agency

- Pre-KPE number of monthly auto policies sold: 4
- Average annual policy premium: $1,500
- Average length of policy: 3.5 years
- Average total premium over policy lifetime: $5,250
- Commission to agency: 15%
- Pre-KG margin per auto policy sold: $787.50
- Pre-KG annual auto commission: $37,800 (4 policies per month x $787.50 x 12 months)

Indirect Opportunity Key Initiative: Get service agents to increase the no-obligation referral *"quotes for auto"* from 3% to 30%.

Direct Opportunity Key Initiative: Increase conversion of *"follow-up sales specialists"* from 20% to 30%.

Actual Impact After Full Implementation of KPE

- Revised number of monthly auto policies sold: 50
- Average annual policy premium: $1,500
- Average length of policy: 3.5 years
- Average total premium over policy lifetime: $5,250

- Commission to agency: 15%
- Margin per auto policy sold: $787.50
- Revised annual auto commission: $472,500
  (50 policies per month x $787.50 x 12 months)
- Increase in company margin: +$434,700 ($472,500 - $37,800)

Winning End Results

- ✔ **1150% increase in auto policy-generated annual profit!**
  ($434,700/$37,800)
- ✔ **Happier direct-selling employees**
- ✔ **Happier indirect-selling employees (service referrers)**
- ✔ **Happier managers**
- ✔ **Happier customers**
- ✔ **Happier primary owners and partners**

⮑ Case Closed!

Once you identify your true potential influence, you will find that the Frontline revenue opportunities within your grasp are overwhelming and inspiring. It then becomes critical that you share this financial epiphany with *all* levels in your organization, to secure total buy-in. If you don't make sure it happens with a personal and visible commitment, you will mute the enthusiasm and subsequent motivation needed to bring all of this to fruition.

Depending on your current financial situation, this impact can improve profits, double them, or, in many cases, be the *only* profit!

⮑ Profit You Can Control

I hope this chapter has provided more insight on the revenue potential that exists in the Frontline business world. The exciting thing is that this revenue is within grasp and within your control.

Let's face it—there are many factors in business you simply cannot control, including the following:

- The state of the economy

- New market competitors of all sizes that move into your territory

- Massive advertising campaigns by your competitors

- Market price devaluations from your competitors that force you to lower prices

- Macroeconomic factors such as labor shortages, rising fuel prices, progressive technology, weather, political turmoil, international terrorism or currency devaluations

You have virtually no control over these events! What you do have full control over is how you respond to the above and what you do with your Frontline people. That's your competitive advantage.

So the question is this: Are you going to allow outside factors to determine your future? Or, will you invest in creating a thriving, nearly matchless service-based sales culture that will give you a leg up on your competitors?

Are you going to view your Frontline as a "necessary evil"? Or will you begin to look at it as the one competitive advantage you actually have total control over?

> "Man who waits for roast duck to fly into mouth must wait very, very long time."
> — Chinese Proverb

Will your managers and Frontline people remain "task masters," "processors" and "order takers?" Or will they become "mini-businesses" within your larger business who are worthy of attention and development?

Make the right choice and you will create a team with the ability of caring for your customers and the power to generate unprecedented profits.

KHOURY KEY TAKEAWAYS
CHAPTER 2

Map out all the customer touch points and the related sales opportunities.

✔ Most companies have over four to six sales opportunity customer interactions

NO-BULL KNOW HOW!

Understand and appreciate the difference in the sales management process of the following customer touch points in your business:

✔ Indirect sales opportunities, such as a bank teller, a cashier or a receptionist

✔ Direct sales opportunities, such as an insurance agent, a server, or leasing specailist

✔ A combination of both

BANKING ON IT!

Study the various case studies to apply what is appropriate to your operation and make the revenue case for your organization:

✔ Apply the sales numbers of your top 10% producers to the average of your location; you will find that the spread is usually a 50% difference in performance.

✔ Apply the sales numbers of your top 10% producers to the bottom 10% producers; you will find that the spread is usually a 100% difference in performance.

✔ Put these numbers together and you will find that most Frontline organizations have a conservative 30% upside or more.

✔ Your personal visible commitment is critical to achieving these goals.

Great companies go for peak performance, not relative improvement

*Understand and appreciate the role of your Frontline as the vehicle that can transform your bottom line. Selling at the Frontline is **one of the few primary profit factors in business that you can, in fact, control.***

CHAPTER 3

SELLING A SALES CULTURE

"Opportunities are rarely lost. The other fellow takes those you miss."

— *Anonymous*

Whether you are a division within a large organization or a small single-site operator, implementing the kind of culture change envisioned by the Khoury Performance Equation is a huge undertaking. After all, achieving performance potential for many companies means changing "how things are done" on a daily basis—and that's a big deal, no matter how big or small your company!

The challenges are many. From the misconception of colleagues that this is "easy stuff," to different departments and people that will *not* want your help. You will find many resisters along the way and many, in fact, may actively work against you to "protect their turf." Add to that a group of managers that already has its hands full, and perhaps another group that has its collective ego on the line, and you now have a small mountain to climb!

In this chapter I discuss some key concepts relating to the KPE that will help shed more light on its benefits, as well as on those challenges you'll face in selling it internally. These insights will add to your knowledge bank, giving you the ammunition and overall knowledge you will need to battle and overcome the challenges to achieve a winning end result that is now within your reach.

➋ The Commodity Trap

In our increasingly global and competitive economy, businesses in all industries must try to reduce one of their biggest variable costs: labor. To do so, they are constantly searching for the latest and greatest technology to replace the work of people.

Of course, there are numerous situations where machines can perform better than humans. You can look at any modern assembly line and see the merits of automation.

However, there is another, potentially darker side to this equation: *commoditization*. This is an inability to distinguish yourself in the service arena! Reduced human interaction with your customers puts your businesses at risk by leveling the playing field and turning your service closer to a commodity.

Once this happens it will always be a challenge to charge any more for your products and services, and it will be difficult, if not impossible, to undo.

IS YOUR COMPANY RELATIONAL OR TRANSACTIONAL?

When you are booking a hotel today over the internet, can you "feel" the difference between one five-star hotel in New York City and another? Of course not. This changes however, if you are on the phone and you have an enthusiastic and motivated salesperson on the other end of the line, describing the property's distinct benefits. In those moments, that representative *is* the hotel. It is in those situations that a company becomes "relational" versus "transactional," producing a huge flashpoint of advantage.

Need proof? Consider these revealing responses from a study of over 9,000 customers in the retail arena. They were asked, "What is the *most* important thing you look for in a shopping experience?"

- *41.4% of participants wanted knowledgeable and helpful salespeople.*
- *27.0% of participants wanted courteous, caring and friendly staff.*
- *18.3% of participants wanted low prices and product information.*
- *8.8% of participants wanted merchandise that is easy to find.*
- *4.5% of participants wanted a fast check out.*

Source: When Customers Talk … Turn What They Tell You Into Sales, T.Scott Gross & BIG Research, Dearborn Publishing 2005, page 142

As you can see, a full 72.9% of what people are looking for is impacted by your Frontline. This is a human asset you have so much control over influencing through the Khoury Performance Equation.

Advantage: Your People!

Recent customer service studies have shown that the increasing dependence on and infiltration of technology into our lives has a created a universal hunger for more personal interaction.

The brands that recognize this and have a method of capitalizing on this trend will be able to position themselves ahead of their competitors for years to come. Customers want to know that their business is valued. There is no better way to accomplish that than through your team at the Frontline.

Your Team is Your Trump Card

Starbucks founder Howard Schultz probably said it best when he told *Business Week,* "We have no patent and no secret sauce. The only competitive edge we have is the relationship we have built with our people and they have built with the customer." Although Starbucks may have experienced some recent challenges, it remains one of the worlds most successful and admired companies. The notion that their business is about people is not just a mantra or big talk.

Schultz went on to say that they were in the people business—that although they sold coffee it was really about a human connection. "We've been able to crack the code at creating an environment where people are treated well," he said. "They're respected and they're valued. Customers can come in and see it's a different kind of environment."

Schultz understands that their explosive expansion, the economy, and fierce competition have all caused part of the challenges Starbucks faces today. However, he believes that the key to continued success, to reigning as "number one," is in having an *emotional attachment* with customers.

The critical points that are made here can shape your entire mindset. Say your company is investing huge sums of money in infrastructure costs, sales and marketing, operations, administration, and their related areas. This investment has been put forth to make the phone ring and to bring customer opportunities into your store or business.

In a sales environment, if the Frontline is simply *"processing"* those customers, it may be leaving a majority or all of your profit on the table. In the process, it is also shortchanging customers by not letting them know about your best products and services or giving them the opportunity to enjoy them.

Ask yourself if that is still acceptable to you and your shareholders. Then, ask if you want order-takers and taskmasters, or if you want professional, motivated salespeople. Do you want bodies on your sales floor, or do you want a finely tuned Frontline Profit Machine?

➋ The Service Chain

Ultimately, the KPE system is about service. Letting this concept sink down to the organization's structure means understanding the following:

- The owner/general manager's primary customers are their direct reports.
- The midlevel managers' primary customers are their Frontline managers.
- The Frontline manager's primary customers are their Frontline salespeople.

In this scenario, servicing your primary customer becomes the number-one sales priority.

As such, the old auto-cratic, aggressive top-down management model has become outdated and obsolete. The days of bringing the boss "a cup of coffee" are over. We live in a new age.

> From Disney to Ritz Carlton to Southwest Airlines … study after study proves that happy employees = productive employees = happy external customers. This means that service success flows from the bottom of the organizational chain up, rather than from the top down.

People have choices about what to do and who to work for. If they don't, they may stick around, but I promise you, you won't get the best out of them. In today's business world you serve the coffee, you put on an apron and BBQ for the Frontline, you thank them for their service and commitment to your company. *You serve the people that serve your customers.*

Today, organizations that want a vibrant Frontline service-based sales culture must shift from their entire organization serving the president, CEO, or owner, to *the entire organization serving the end customer.* (See Figure 3-1.)

Figure 3-1: The progressive service-based sales organization.

This can happen only by concentrating heavy resources in the area where they can do the most good: Your service and sales personnel and their immediate management teams.

➋ Selling the KPE Blueprint Internally

So now you believe in the importance of creating a sales culture in your organization. The key word here is *belief!* You believe that the upside is tremendous for your company and your employees. You believe that this is truly a win for your customers and your co-workers, and a great opportunity for you to deliver unquestionable and quantifiable value to your organization.

If you are the CEO, the COO, the business owner, regional manager, location manager or salesperson, selling this program internally requires that you effectively:

1. Quantify the opportunity	5. Get buy-in and ownership for it
2. Understand it	6. Implement it
3. Create the vision for it	7. Manage it
4. Communicate it	8. Maintain it

Great companies think big but act small. Great managers think big and act where they can. The position you hold within your organization will only limit your initial scope of influence. Be assured that as your results grow and get noticed, so will your power to lead change.

- If you run a location, you can implement this program in your store.
- If you run a department within your location, you can take major elements of this program and create dynamic influences within that department.
- If you are a salesperson who sees "the light," you can sell your boss on implementing key elements of this program, for the benefit of your company, your co-workers and yourself.

The implementation of this program and the consequent revenue improvement will provide for an advantageous test that can only provide further opportunity for you and your team.

Yes! If you believe in it and have the passion, conviction and unwavering commitment to see it through, you can sell it, regardless of your position in the organization.

➔ Not So Simple

Is all this easy? Absolutely not.

Does it look simple and easy? Yes, but looks can be deceiving.

Are most companies good at this? Many think they are, but the truth is most are generally awful at it.

So why does creating a high-performing Frontline seem so simple? On the surface it appears so because people assume the following:

- The training department alone can do it.
- The human resources department can take care of it.
- "John's a good manager." He can fix it by himself.
- The business is well run in other areas, so all that is needed is greater *focus*.
- There is little understanding, conviction or belief in the amount of real upside and small and/or cyclical increases are easy to achieve.
- Frontline positions have never been truly valued or looked at as critical.
- The transaction itself is not complex.
- The top brass does not really understand the Frontline and can't generally relate to the people on it.
- A few tasks can fix it, perhaps training, or a good incentive plan, or better hires.

Half the battle is to understand what the task at hand *is* and what it will actually take to get it done. Shattering these limiting perceptions is a critical first step in building a high-performance sales culture.

As I will mention again and again, it is terrific news that this is not easy stuff! If it were, everyone would do it and there would be no competitive edge or significant money in it.

Recalibrating Management

> "The key is not to prioritize what is on your schedule, but to schedule your priorities."
>
> — Steven Covey

Let's start with the first of many challenges you will need to overcome. This one is at the top of the list.

Most Frontline managers have an operations-based mindset that naturally becomes very task-oriented. It says, "If I perform these specific functions, then I have done my job." These duties include completing general paperwork, scheduling, and actions such as conference calls and running reports.

These are all functions which, in many cases, are done in isolation away from their employees and customers. Although these actions are important, too many managers use them to insulate themselves from the point of sale, where the crucial actions happen and where their presence is most needed.

I am not diminishing other responsibilities or their value. These tasks are important, perhaps even critical, to the efficient functioning of your business. However, at the

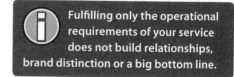

Fulfilling only the operational requirements of your service does not build relationships, brand distinction or a big bottom line.

end of the day, they give your organization very little edge. Companies managed this way typically have service results with their paying customers that are, at best, equal to that of, or slightly below, their average competitor.

Perpetual Poor Planning

We often get the comment that "all this sounds good on paper," but it is "impractical in real life" when considering the other internal demands placed on the average field manager's day-to-day schedule.

You may be asking, "How can we do all of this when we are already short-staffed?" Many see their own leaders frequently bogged down just attempting to meet some basic operational needs. This is a real conundrum common to most companies across most industries.

The Frontline manager's job is one of the most time-pressured and important in an organization. Many managers we encounter are actually driven by (and addicted to) the ongoing drama of working in a perpetually frenetic and harried manner.

When they are not handling their basic tasks, they are bouncing from emergency to emergency, while regarding their continual and intense urgency as a badge of honor. In reality, this is a result of perpetual poor planning and/or general management weakness. In many cases, the fault is not theirs. It is caused by the culture they work in. It is often simply the result of not being given the tools, the training, the reasons, the guidance, or the direction necessary to improve.

Recalibrate and Reprioritize

Look at the tasks that you and your managers spend your time on. Then ask yourself if ultimately that time is *well* spent. Here are some typical tasks that can stifle your sales focus and profits:

- Compiling unnecessary reports, or creating them too often relative to the actual frequency that is needed
- Responding to an email on which you were Cc'd (not the intended primary recipient)
- Creating and changing employee schedules
- Participating in company conference calls that generate little or no tangible value
- Attending meetings that are scheduled, but are no longer necessary
- Addressing common operational issues that would be better handled through delegation
- Focusing on non-revenue tasks as your "primary" or "core" responsibility

In most companies there is an urgent need to recalibrate and reprioritize daily management tasks.

Addressing inefficiencies in an organization could fill a series of books on its own. Get clarity on what your managers need to spend time on. Look at what really matters and consider:

- Simplifying keys reports
- Identifying new metrics that reveal crucial data on your strengths and opportunities
- Understanding how a manager's hourly activities impact the company environment that influence how your employees serve your customers

So how is all this done? You need to make prudent trade-offs that will reduce low-yield management activities and replace them with those that are more vitally strategic.

THE POWER OF PRESENCE

Another critical first step is for upper management to understand and believe that managers generate the most value to the organization when they spend time with their staff and clientele. When this happens, many of the "operational tasks" now inhibiting

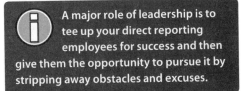

A major role of leadership is to tee up your direct reporting employees for success and then give them the opportunity to pursue it by stripping away obstacles and excuses.

the peak service and sales effort will be redistributed, reduced in scope, or in many instances, eliminated altogether.

When your managers invest their time with the Frontline, many non-direct revenue tasks start to disappear. This then frees up more time for them to drive performance because managers spend:

- Less time screening and interviewing new applicants because turnover is down

- Less time doing things themselves because they can delegate some "tasks" to the experienced Frontline employees they have now developed

- Less time scheduling as a performance-based system becomes acceptable and easier to manage

- Less time with unhappy employees

- Less time with unhappy customers

- Less time dealing with weak sales performance and a weak P & L while always trying to rationalize it to upper management

OFF THE SIDELINES AND INTO THE GAME

Reaching potential is about getting the most out of your people and resources. Everyone wins when your managers are able to spend more time where it really counts: the Frontline.

Show me a restaurant, retail store, or airline/hotel check-in counter where the managers are absent, and I can assure you that you are looking at a business that is performing marginally, at best. If you want superior performance, you need to assess the level of sales support presence that exists at your company. Ponder the following questions:

- How do managers motivate and inspire your team members while they are doing reports in the back office?

- How do they build a positive relationship with your employees and earn their trust if they are nowhere to be found?

- How can they welcome your customers, ensure their needs are being met or understand the challenges of serving them if they are constantly "out of sight" in "the back" or participating on their third "cost-cutting" conference call this month with the corporate office?

Want to give your business a great chance to succeed? *Get your managers out of the back and up to the front!*

KHOURY PERFORMANCE STORY

Making the Case over a Nice House Red

A few years back, 225 managers from Romano's Macaroni Grill nationwide led a toast by each raising a glass of their house Chianti. What was the occasion? Did the popular restaurant chain turn 50? Was it someone's birthday? Was it a toast to acknowledge an earth shattering accomplishment?

Sales Milestone

}

The management team was celebrating the chain's sale of its 100 millionth glass of house wine. Not only was the 100 millionth glass a sales milestone, but it was a testament to what a Frontline Profit Machine can do to boost revenue and provide a great customer experience.

In his autobiography *Food For Thought,* Phillip J. Romano, the creator of the restaurant chain wrote, **"from an economics stand point I did not care if we made money on the food because I was in the wine business."**

Here's to the bottom line

}

The average Macaroni Grill posted $4 million a year in sales, over 25% of the total came from wine sales. The beautiful story behind the $1 million in wine sales was that a whopping $890,000 dropped to the bottom line. Their cost was only 11% on house wines. Much of the wine that is sold is done so on the honor system that results in a warm feeling and added sales. A large wine jug is placed on the table and customers pour as they please.

A great deal of thought and effort goes into this chain's recipe for success! It is not surprising that Macaroni grill today has won the coveted "Choice of Chains" award for five years in a row. Great food, jugs of wine, and a Frontline service and sales machine make for a great trio.

➋ Shattering the Myths

Let me start with the biggest myth of all:

Myth: Excellent training is the solution

Fact: Excellent training by itself is overrated

Why? Because companies that have a good or even a great training program often feel that they are already doing all they can to sufficiently and completely support the sales effort. In an attempt to perpetuate their sales programs, some invest further in online training and expensive technology to provide an ongoing influence after an initial live classroom program. Others even go as far as dedicating additional trainers to specifically focus on the sales improvement effort.

As a result of all this, ownership may believe they are doing everything in their power to get their staff and organization in position to achieve their stated goals. Their perception is that they have reached the "support mountaintop" when they have actually just begun the climb!

One of the first things an existing sales leader must acknowledge is that he or she does not have all of the answers. A common misconception most CEOs we work with have is they feel that training alone is the solution.

The fundamental problem is that training by itself is not enough to transform a culture ... It is not even close to enough! In most cases, from a pure total opportunity perspective, it fails miserably in achieving the organization's true revenue-generating potential.

TRAINING IS ONLY PART OF THE SOLUTION

Outside of the training and human resources departments, many others in leadership circles often perceive that knowledge in the sales arena is "common knowledge." Hence, they again see training as *the* comprehensive solution. The thinking goes something like this: Just give the Frontline some training, some sales phrases, some product knowledge, get the managers to focus on it, and the job will be done.

I have learned to not guarantee too many things in life but I will guarantee

> ⓘ At best, sales training by itself changes behavior in a small percentage of people for a short period of time. In the majority of cases, once the novelty of the sales training has worn off, so does its effectiveness.

this: *Training alone will not get the job done!*

After a short "fool's-gold" burst of higher performance, the results in-variably cascade back down to their original levels as people return to their embedded habits. Then, they only spike again with the next training initiative or seminar. Sound familiar? You are not alone. In fact, you are in the majority! Frustrating, isn't it?

From Selling Training to Selling Results

We've been there. My firm at one time was mired in the training mindset and made those same mistakes. Our core offering in our early years was primarily oriented solely around training. We delivered seminars and on-site follow-up training. That's it. We thought our clients wanted training, so that is what we gave them.

Even though it was limited in scope, many of our clients enjoyed substantial results and a fantastic short-term return on their investment from our work. Others got a quick education and became believers in the impact and power of their Frontline. However, with the exception of the most advanced operators that implemented some of the KPE elements on their own, their results for the most part eventually deteriorated over time.

At some point, we realized that we did not want to be just another training company that delivered good seminars, since many successful companies already did that. We understood that customers were buying only one thing from us, and that one thing was *not training!* They were buying *bottom-line results!*

Since then, we have worked tirelessly to help clients break this gut-wrenching cycle of up-and-down roller coaster performance.

Use that mindset to sell this program internally in your organization.

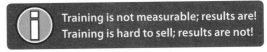

Training is not measurable; results are!
Training is hard to sell; results are not!

A PERSONAL BUSINESS TRANSFORMATION

So how did we get results once we realized that they were not attained by training alone? We went to work and continued to develop a system that was capable of delivering these results, regardless of the sales situation.

With time, a lot of effort and a lot of fine-tuning, we identified the key elements that make improved performance stick. They became the base on which the Khoury Performance Equation was built. Once we discovered its power to strengthen and protect our clients' *long-term results,* the tide for our business turned ... *just as it will for you if you embrace its elements and work to implement them.*

> If you can measure it, you can promise it! If you then deliver on it, customers will pay you for it, and in many cases, pay you well! This was true for us and it will be true for you.

➔ Blowing Up More Myths

While we are blasting away at many of the sacred cows of Frontline sales performance, here are our opinions on a few other perceived "whole" solutions and what we have learned:

Myth: Commission plans are the solution

Fact: Commission plans by themselves are overrated

Myth: Measurement and reporting effectively is the solution

Fact: Measurement and reporting, on their own, are overrated

Myth: Better communication is the solution

Fact: Better communication by itself is overrated

Myth: Building strong relationships with your team is the solution

Fact: Strong relationships by themselves are overrated

Myth: Recognition is the solution

Fact: Recognition on its own is overrated

Myth: Best-practice standards are the solution

Fact: Best-practice standards by themselves are overrated

Myth: Recruitment is the solution

Fact: Recruitment by itself is overrated

The implementation of the KPE is the "whole" solution ... and that's a fact!

An Interdependent Solution

All of these actions are, in fact, critical, but they cannot stand alone to ensure peak sales performance. We often come across companies who perform one, two, or three of these areas well and feel they are doing all they can. This false sense of security can so shroud a leadership team that even when a clear case for larger opportunity is made, they just cannot see it.

Capitalizing on sales opportunities requires the sales management team to not only be skilled in train-ing. It requires expertise in

> ℹ️ Never confuse doing "everything you can" with "everything that can be done." They are usually vastly different, and produce vastly different results.

incentive program creation (for both sales and management), recruitment and selection among a host of other best practices.

It requires extensive expertise in defining the right sales metrics and designing simple and effective reports. It requires experience in performance management, leadership development, team building, personal development, quality assurance, public speaking, and sales process development.

Since most training functions address only a fractional portion of this, they end up with fractional results. What's worse is that they struggle mightily and end up discouraged because they cannot get higher sales performance to "stick." As a result, the organization falls far short of its peak potential, eventually resigning itself to mediocrity and rationalization.

> ℹ️ Comprehensive employee team behavior can be improved long-term only through a holistic sales culture change.

➡ Performance Killers

> "No executive has ever suffered because his subordinates were strong and effective."
> — Peter Drucker

Before you move forward with implementing the KPE internally, you need to consider a few more challenges you will face so that you can be prepared to handle them. These include lack of faith in this new idea among your company or division leaders, being blocked by a skeptical or threatened boss, as well as the delusion that there is nothing to be learned from other companies or industries.

Performance Killer #1
* **Lack of Knowledge = Lack of Belief = Lack of Results**

The lack of understanding and belief in the real upside potential of the Frontline often draws leaders away from investing in their team's performance improvement. But do they have the correct perspective? Are they getting the right story from those around them? The leaders who pull the trigger on performance improvement budgets and establish the cultural vision for the company traditionally get their information from their field managers.

Generally speaking, the bigger the company, the more territorial the various departments can be. The training and human resources departments are usually at the top of that list. In many cases even the operations departments can often be defensive as well.

Frequently, the larger the business, the more removed upper management. If these two factors are present and these departments are reporting they are "doing their best" you will most likely find that they are rolling out nothing more than "the latest, greatest" management workshop, which will soon become nothing more than a memory.

You are now left with upper management thinking they are doing a good job while *another well-meaning but low-producing initiative sparks, catches fire and flames out.*

Performance Killer #2
* **The Boss**

Whether you are a store manager or a regional manager, understanding the KPE and communicating it to the decision makers is critical. Your boss wants to hear that you are willing to own something and be responsible for it. If you have a boss who feels threatened, perform even better in your current position and earn the opportunity to go to *his* or *her* boss.

There is a sign at Del Frisco's Steakhouse in Orlando sitting right over the bar that says: "Do the right thing and fear no one." I love that line and share it often with my team.

 Creating a Frontline Profit Machine in your company, region, store or department *is* the right thing to do.

(☠) Performance Killer #3
• Not Learning from Others

The best business schools will tell you that as long as it is legal, you should take a good idea and copy it!

Regardless of how strong you feel that your organization is in sales and sales management, imagine the following scenario. Let us say you had the opportunity to leave your business for two years, knowing it would be fine without you. Then, over that period, you did nothing but focus on researching the world's best Frontline-selling organizations with the mission of extracting the very best sales practices from numerous industries, both inside and outside of your current one.

Envision studying the Ruth's Chris Steakhouse chain to see how their Frontline servers maximize wine sales and improve the ticket average in their restaurants while providing exceptional service. How do they recruit and select strong, caring, sales-oriented people? What process do they use to increase per-ticket averages without being heavy-handed and turning away business? How do they train the individuals initially and recurrently? How do they build their product knowledge? How do they provide management incentives so their leadership team will drive the effort on a daily basis? How do they measure individual performance? Now visualize doing this in Las Vegas, in New York City, in Denver and in Dallas.

Then, do the exact same thing with Avis Car Rental, asking similar questions, but now in a car rental context. How are they so successful in Tulsa, Los Angeles, Chicago, Vancouver and Dublin? Then, view the processes that exist in the retail arena with companies such as Rocky Mountain Chocolate Factory, or in the automotive services industry with Canadian Tire.

You then analyze the travel and tourism industry secrets of phone sales with Sandals and Beaches Resorts in the Caribbean and a retail sales culture at a Nordstrom's department store in Seattle.

Now, I have an extremely important question for you: If you were able to perform this exercise, do you think you would learn or encounter anything you might be able to use in your business that you are not doing currently?

As strong as you may be right now, if you had the opportunity to do this, wouldn't you agree that you would amass so much unique and fresh knowledge by studying these great companies that you would return after the two years and completely revolutionize your sales effort? Of course you would!

☠ Performance Killer #4
•┄┄┄ Not Getting Out of Your Own Way

Some of the most dynamic CEOs in the country state that remaining teachable is a core reason for their success. Just ask Steve Bennett, former CEO at software giant Intuit.

> *In a Stanford student-organized View from the Top speech on Nov. 18, 2003, Steve Bennett, the dynamic CEO of software-powerhouse Intuit, explained his leadership "road rules."*
>
> *After working in an unrelated field for 23 years, Bennett arrived at Intuit with no software experience and when the company was fighting a battle to reach the $1B threshold, and losing. It was full of "smart employees who didn't know how to get to where they wanted to go," he said.*
>
> *Before beginning the push for the new plateau, his mission focused on how to engage his employees by convincing them they could marry "high performance with a great place to work." But doing so came with behavioral prerequisites like "having a teachable point of view."*
>
> *The desire for change may come easily, but actually creating it in the face of entrenched inertia isn't. "People are natural learners but companies aren't. They have learning disabilities," said Bennett. "Leaders who are successful are great at continuing to learn and have the courage to direct change."*
>
> *A key for Bennett was to shock people from their idea of relative improvement to total potential improvement, terming it the "bullet train that leads to quantum change."*
>
> *What type of "bullet train" did Bennett create? Before leaving in 2008, Intuit had not only achieved the $1 billion mark, but hurdled past the $2 billion one as well.*

The innate weakness of a singular, internally driven strategy is that the people most often charged with the responsibility of moving the service and sales ball forward also possess backgrounds and subsequent ideas that are confined to their own historical industry best practices.

It is okay to admit that you don't know enough about this area. The fact is that some of the most brilliant solutions for overcoming mediocre sales performance in your industry simply do not exist in your industry! Search for them!

☠ Performance Killer #5
• Ego

Management teams often outsource a myriad of services to people and providers with specialized core expertise. Accounting departments use accounting firms to augment their work. Legal departments use outside firms to assist them in all types of projects. Risk management departments use outside security services companies to guard their properties.

> "The intelligent man who is proud of his intelligence is like the condemned man who is proud of his large cell."
>
> — Simone Weil, French philosopher

Yet, when it comes to creating a high-performance sales environment, all of a sudden it is a different story. Seeking sales management expertise from an outside vendor? No way! You hear things like, "Who knows *our* business better than we do?" or "We have been doing this for years" or "Our customers are different; we know how to handle them ourselves."

How's that for irony?

In many cases, even when some managers are clearly shown that they are leaving huge chunks of profit at the Frontline, their ego, defensiveness, or protectiveness sets in, blinding them from valuing any experience or concept that is not their own.

Don't let that defensiveness stop you from pointing out these facts. You sometimes have to build enough pain about the current state of mediocrity to ignite a dramatic change.

☠ Performance Killer #6
• Politics

Internal politics are part of the fabric of many larger companies (and many small ones as well). Those that do have great ideas, and the initiative and energy to follow through with them, get held up in politics and red tape like this:

- The training department is territorial when it comes to employee development.
- The human resource department has to approve the recruitment policy and every local recruitment ad that

advertises for "experienced salespeople" at the Frontline. This often decelerates the process of finding replacements quickly; all while the business is bleeding profit through diminished performance.

- Then, the finance department has to analyze the "new incentive" plan. Although they understand the concept is to pay more out of "found money", they still cannot understand how or why they should pay *those employees* "so much?" It just doesn't seem "right" to them.

- In a smaller company, the general manager tells the boss that he can "take it all on," but he actually ends up doing very little.

➋ A Winner for All

Rationalization of mediocrity clouds the perception of true revenue potential in many companies. When you consider that many decision makers at the top are not well versed

> "Action conquers fear."
> — Peter Nivio Zarlenga,
> business philosopher

on what the Frontline really does, it is easy to understand why most of them overlook this enormous profit opportunity.

The bottom line is that creating a service-based sales culture is a winner for all involved: the customer, the company, its owners and employees. At the end of the day, it is a big win for you if you support it, and a huge opportunity loss that will catch up with you if you do not.

Internalizing the concepts in this book can make you an excellent sales leader. But gaining and possessing this knowledge is useless if it just sits there in your head. You cannot be a great sales *leader* unless you are "leading" someone. You have to do something with the information. And doing something with it may mean that, at some point, you will have to "confront the institution" in your business. That may prove difficult, but trust me, the future results are worth overcoming the challenges you will face, and face down. Great opportunities are within your reach.

Selling a sales culture internally means changing "how things are done"–and that's a big deal! Understand and appreciate that, although the sales process itself may be a simple one, achieving sales potential is not easy stuff.

NO-BULL KNOW HOW!

Understand the following key challenges and opportunities:

Commoditization
- ✔ Automation/technology to reduce labor cost may make it harder to distinguish yourself in the service arena.
- ✔ This makes the human/personal touch that remains even more important to your business.

The service chain
- ✔ Great companies in today's business world focus on their employees first. They serve from the top down to create happy employees and happy customers.

Recalibrate and reprioritize Frontline management duties
- ✔ To increase presence at the Frontline and focus on revenue results
- ✔ To remove obstacles and create a positive sales effect

Shattering the myths to sell a culture
- ✔ Alone and separately, training, commission plans, reports, communication, strong relationships, recognition, sales standards, and/or good recruitment do not work.
- ✔ There is no one magic bullet; they need to all come together to maximize results.

Understand, anticipate and prepare to face all these obstacles, challenges and performance killers
- ✔ Lack of knowledge and belief
- ✔ The insecure boss
- ✔ The "we know it all" disease
- ✔ Getting out of your own way
- ✔ The "not invented here" syndrome
- ✔ Politics and "save my butt" affliction

BANKING ON IT!

When selling anything **the easiest and most powerful thing to sell is bottom-line results.**

PART 2

UNDERSTANDING THE KHOURY PERFORMANCE EQUATION

CHAPTER 4

THE RIGHT ENVIRONMENT FOR MAXIMIZING PROFIT

"You can dream, create, design, and build the most wonderful place in the world ... but it requires people to make the dream a reality."

— Walt Disney

What do GE, Starbucks, Apple, FedEx, and Google have in common? They share the distinction of being in *Fortune's* Top 10 Most Admired Companies of 2008. But, more importantly, they all provide great working environments for their people. These environments foster and encourage development, input, trust, support and opportunities.

These companies empower their people, they believe in them, they reward them and they invest in their development and their personal growth.

On the other hand, it is *not* surprising that three of the least admired companies in people management and customer service—Delta, Northwest and United Airlines—are in an industry that has lost billions in recent years.

The clear connection here is that the happiness and motivation of your employees, especially those on the Frontline, are critical components to your company's success.

Although rare, it is possible to be an average company and be profitable with a mediocre working environment. It is, however, *impossible* to have a great company with sustained growth and profit while dealing with a negative and sluggish company environment.

This chapter details the key environmental factors that are the foundation of the Khoury Performance Equation blueprint. These factors encompass the core of the company sales culture. They also create a consistent base of trust, credibility, respect, and encouragement so that your Frontline salespeople can fully develop their skills.

➋ Nourishing Your Company's Most Valuable Asset

A dead end job. Who wants that? Unfortunately, that is the reality for many workers. They may spend years just going through the motions and putting in minimal effort, or they may quickly seek a more inspiring setting working for someone else. Neither situation will benefit your company's income statement.

The Right Environment is such a simple concept. The truth, however, is that many organizations pay no attention to it at all. A positive environment motivates and harnesses your employees' best efforts to do well. On the other hand, a negative or indifferent environment quickly erodes commitment and spirals performance downward.

➋ A Win-Win Outcome

It is basic human nature: treat your managers well and they will treat your Frontline employees well. If they are happy, they will keep your customers happy, who will then come back and tell their friends.

How successful do you believe this major airline is when the work environment had deteriorated to the point where some of their pilots placed a billboard ad near Philadelphia Airport that broadcast "Our Airline Sucks." What does that say about the environment for that airline and how reassuring it is to the customers who were about to board their planes!

On the other end of the spectrum is Starbucks. Recently its stock price has pulled back in the face of increasing competition and less novelty in the marketplace, but for many years this company was one of American business's greatest success stories. Its stock rose 5,000% (yes, 5,000%) in the 15 years, and a *Fortune* magazine survey ranked the coffee chain as number six among America's Most Admired Companies. Naturally, Starbucks is also well known as one of the best employers to work for. As a result, many well-respected business experts recognize Starbucks as one of the world's best brands.

This is a company that has taken a very simple commodity—coffee—and built a unique and exciting "experience" around it. And, it doesn't just serve its customers. Its main focus is creating a great environment for its own employees whom the company calls "partners."

Clearly, successful management teams like those at Starbucks fully understand the power of a "people-centered" culture. Leaders know that creating The Right Environment for their "partners" is *the* most important thing they can do to continue to grow and be successful.

Environment: A Foundation for Success

An environment that motivates people accounts for much of the difference between a high-performing organization and one that merely muddles along or languishes, delivering substandard results. Focus on building a great environment and watch your team and your business grow and prosper!

People innately know if their work is respected and valued. Conversely, they also know when they are being disregarded or used solely to fulfill some unseen corporate objective. Creating The Right Environment for unbridled success demands a *holistic* approach.

This allows your people's needs to be met now and in the long term. This allows them to truly look forward to coming to work, enthused and empowered to make a profound difference in your company's success.

You Need More than Money in an Envelope

Performance-based financial rewards are certainly a key factor in success. In fact, I will address the subject in more detail a little later in this book. However, creating The Right Environment requires more than compensation.

Many people may not understand that money in an envelope is simply a medium of exchange, a specific number of dollars given for a specific number of hours or days worked. That's the limitation. After the period is completed and the payment for that labor has been disbursed, the two parties are, in essence, even. The employee has fulfilled his or her commitment to perform, and the company has reciprocated by fulfilling its monetary obligation.

This trade, in and of itself, is exactly that a trade. Standing alone, compensation will not elicit the very best from your team member. On the contrary, employees in this situation most often default to what is "the path of least resistance," performing only at the minimum levels required to earn their pay. *It takes a higher purpose to drive someone to exceed consistently.*

 Money may satisfy an immediate need, but it will never, by itself, bind an individual to an organization's long-term vision.

⮎ The Right Environment and Why They Quit

Leigh Branham, author of *The 7 Hidden Reasons Employees Leave,* actually identifies 57 preventable reasons for voluntary turnover. When he started looking for common denominators and "root causes," he boiled it all down to only four fundamental human needs that are not being met when employees call it quits:

- The need for trust
- The need for hope
- The need to feel a sense of worth
- The need to feel competent

People need to understand that there is an opportunity for them to achieve their potential, both personally and professionally. There are opportunities to grow, to build their abilities, to contribute personally and meaningfully to the leadership team and to the company's success. But the employer needs to help its employees realize this and bring it to fruition.

Once employees reach this level of commitment—where they trust others and feel trusted, hopeful, valued and competent—they will achieve incredible new levels of productivity.

⮎ Eight Building Blocks for Success

Peak-performing organizations share common environmental characteristics. At the heart is an understanding of what is truly important to managers and Frontline employees. This knowledge provides a simple and useful basis to create a business and sales culture that addresses them.

Ask yourself this simple question: "What steps can I take to ensure that my employees feel more connected to our organizational mission?" The answers reveal actions that fall into well-defined spheres. Link these areas together and you get a clear picture of what it takes to build a successful working environment that drives people to give their best, and not just what is minimally expected.

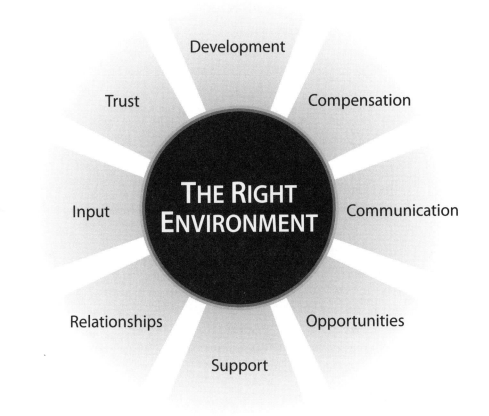

Figure 4-1: The core elements that make up The Right Environment revolve primarily around a set of needs that are common to most employees in most organizations.

COMMON SENSE?

Our research, and more importantly, our experience, has identified eight *interdependent* areas as the keys to unleashing peak employee productivity. (See Figure 4-1.) Collectively, they define how your company expresses its respect for its managers and Frontline staff. You can understand each of these areas better from the employee point of view as critical questions that shape how they feel about what they do.

1. Development	How will the company help me improve my professional and selling skills so I can be more successful?
2. Compensation	Will the company pay me what I am worth relative to my profit contribution?
3. Communication	Will the company keep me informed about my performance, the company's performance along with key issues and trends that affect our business and customer focus?
4. Opportunities	Is there a career path and an opportunity for growth and advancement? A promotion, a management position, potential partnership, etc.? Are there opportunities for me to grow financially as my skills develop?
5. Support	What tools and material support will the company provide to help me do my job better? Is management willing to do the things they are asking me to do?
6. Relationships	Is the company culture designed to build and maintain positive relationships between my managers, my co-workers and me?
7. Input	Do I have the opportunity to provide feedback and make suggestions that can contribute to the company's growth?
8. Trust	Does the company seek to build a culture of trust between executives, managers and Frontline employees? Can I trust my boss? Does my boss trust me?

Figure 4-2: These eight areas are the keys to unleashing peak employee productivity.

Common sense? Sure, but as the saying goes, it is pretty surprising how uncommon common sense can be.

> The beauty of creating this environment, one in which employees will thrive, is that in most cases, you can! It is your business and the decision and the power to carry out all eight of these elements is yours.

KHOURY PERFORMANCE STORY

The Right Environment in Action

Southwest Airlines founder and CEO Emeritus Herb Kelleher has built and led a company that has weathered all the storms the airline industry could throw at him. They have had incredible success in every one of their 36 years of existence and are consistently named as one of Fortunes most admired companies.

> Kelleher often says, *"Your people come first, and if you treat them right, they'll treat customer's right, and the customers will come back, and that'll make the shareholders happy."*

The man *Chief Executive* magazine named the CEO of the Century makes it sound exceedingly simple. As he notes, "We are in the customer service business and we happen to be an airline." In what is a traditionally "a commodity" like business, he knows that the environment he has created at Southwest has ingrained a culture of "dedication, devotion, and loyalty"; the result is a competitive edge that cannot easily be duplicated by the rest of the industry.

Southwest has been very creative in identifying ways to keep this environment alive and thriving while it has become one of the nation's top five carriers.

For example, it formed a culture committee for the sole purpose of "doing whatever it takes to keep the Southwest culture alive." Employees on the "Internal Customer Care Team" do things like send out over 75,000 cards to colleagues to recognize birthdays, anniversaries and the birth of children. Southwest does not just talk about making employees number one—they do it!

Is the effort and resources to create and maintain an environment that will create happy, productive employees worth it? Just ponder the fact that if you had invested just $1,000 in Kelleher's fledgling venture in 1972, you would have $1.4 million dollars today!

You Are in Control

As basic as they may seem, very few companies actually focus on implementing these elements, even though it takes much less work to sustain them for ongoing success.

- Creating The Right Environment provides the foundation for a business and sales culture that is positive and productive.
- It creates an atmosphere that is genuine and sincere.
- It removes excuses and builds a certain level of obligation between the company, its managers and its Frontline employees.
- It is an environment that sets a higher standard, brings hope to employees that may perceive their position as "limited," "dead end" or, at worst, a "temporary stepping stone" toward another career path.

If There's a Will ...

Every organization has the ability to create The Right Environment. You do not have to be reborn as Nordstrom or Google to have this positive culture. It simply requires a vision, a desire and a blueprint.

The willingness to create The Right Environment has to start at the top. This does not mean that as an owner, a general manager or a sales executive you need to stop everything you are doing and only work on your company's culture. It does, however, mean that you need to be initially involved and engaged in addressing the elements of the KPE blueprint for your organization. You then need to support, endorse, and continue to monitor its development, making it a high priority in your hierarchy of responsibility.

⮡ 1. Development

It is human nature to want to learn and to grow personally and professionally. Investing in the education of your employees does more than allow you to capitalize on their newly refined skills; it creates tethers of reciprocal commitment that compensation alone cannot.

> "When all is said and done, teaching is what I try to do for a living. Truth is, I have always liked teaching."
>
> — Jack Welch, former CEO, General Electric

Today's Frontline salesperson could be tomorrow's group manager or division executive. By providing access to learning, your company is making an investment in its current performance and long-term future.

Professional development is a valuable undertaking for any company. The rewards in terms of employee commitment and loyalty are tremendous.

Different companies have varying budgets for employee development. Often this variability is due to industry norms and/or the value that upper management places on investing in employee growth. These budgets often range from 0% to 5% of company revenue. Most companies, however, default to the lower end of this scale due to their inability to directly quantify returns on these investments. As a result, these organizations leave uncounted millions of dollars on the table annually due to employee ineffectiveness, apathy, or both.

Employee development comes in different forms, from good, old-fashioned one-on-one time, to professional associations, Internet bulletin boards and formal certification courses among many other tracks. In most cases, it is a good idea to utilize a combination of various methods.

ONE-ON-ONE TIME

Great managers understand that they can multiply their efforts by the number of employees reporting to them if those employees can duplicate their own actions. Here, one-on-one time given to educate and develop staff, and to provide direction, can be invaluable, especially when focused on these key areas:

- Key performance metrics
- Accomplishments
- Challenges
- Opportunities
- Customer feedback
- Support needed

Frontline managers, at a minimum, should talk daily with their direct reports, and facilitate monthly formal development sessions with each one. Although this requires time commitment, in the end it actually frees up *more* time as the reporting team strengthens and becomes less dependent on management to resolve many "common sense" decisions.

As an extra bonus, the additional improvements in trust, empowerment and communication generated from this attention will lead to more appreciative and committed team members.

PROFESSIONAL EDUCATION

Investing in professional education can take many forms. You can support employees in Ivy League business school graduate programs, or you can help them get an A.A. degree from the local community college.

A good option is also to send your team to educational seminars. Choose some that are business-related; others can be for personal development. Employees often value personal development seminars even more as they are an investment in their own growth and future success. Seminars on such topics as business etiquette, image and money management are always received extremely well.

Committing yourself to employee development, whether it is spending $75,000 for an MBA program or coordinating free local seminars, is an investment in your business. Define a process to integrate it into your business, budget for it and communicate its importance to every team member in your organization.

CONVENTIONS AND TRADE ASSOCIATIONS

Consider allowing more of your employees to attend industry-specific events that bring together the leaders in your industry. The educational sessions and association with like-minded professionals often stimulate new ideas while helping you address challenges through the past experiences of others.

LEARNING PATH AND CERTIFICATION

One of the most powerful learning tools is professional certification. However, this track will serve you better if you first have in place clearly defined job descriptions with skill prerequisites. These will put you in position to develop recommended learning paths or a series of educational activities for your managers and employees.

Cisco, the computer-networking giant, made employee certification a cornerstone of its business strategy. This is not surprising given the high-tech focus of the company and the level of specialized education many of their job categories require. What is really extraordinary about the Cisco approach is that they turned education and certification for employees, partners, and independent consultants into a profit center. The end result has been a true win-win for everyone involved.

BUSINESS BOOK CLUBS

Book clubs are a great idea for keeping your business environment exciting and creative. Promote business books that you feel are interesting, captivating, and valuable. Encourage your employees to read and prepare one-page reports on them. Keep your staff focused on current business thinking and reinforce the lessons learned in the books at staff and management meetings.

Many current titles are released in both print and e-book format. There are subscription services that offer digests of popular business books that are available both in print and audio format. Encourage your people to listen to them on their iPods or other portable listening devices during their daily commute.

ONLINE RESEARCH AND INDUSTRY BULLETIN BOARDS

If budgetary constraints just do not permit your company to invest in distance or formal training modules, consider the Internet. It is often an overlooked wellspring of potential learning. Most industry trade magazines and associations sponsor specific online bulletin boards where members (usually for free) can post questions, solutions and ideas on best practices.

It may be difficult or embarrassing for you to contact another industry leader to talk about a specific employee issue, but online you can ask these questions discreetly and privately. In that regard, the Internet provides a very safe portal.

Of course, when someone provides input, you should vet it for potential bias and true expertise. Ensure their "recommendations" are anchored in past experience, not concept. Check their background and ask questions about how they arrived at that solution. Also, always seek a second or third opinion from different online sources.

2. Compensation

If the compensation plan is performance-based and designed to clearly deliver the right return on investment, then everyone wins.

The right commission plan focuses on rewarding those that service and sell customers. It is a key factor to improving sales performance. With focus, attention and feedback, well-trained and motivated employees can increase sales on the Frontline by 30% or more.

The right commission plan can alter salespeoples' behavior. They soon get used to the "$1,000 commission check" and it becomes part of their budget for their new car payment. *Soon, sales and good performance become a necessity and not an option.*

Incentives create opportunities and reinforcement for the individual to excel. The incentive amount as a relative percentage of base salary is also critical. If the base pay is too high compared to the performance-based portion, it will not motivate someone to exert the added extraordinary effort required for the perceived menial improvement in compensation. On the other hand, if a compensation plan is too incentive-to-salary laden, it may be harder to attract the right people or lead many of them to be too "pushy" with your customers. You need a balance, one crafted with great diligence, care, and concern.

Financial rewards can be offered in a variety of ways:

- Hourly, salary or overtime
- Incentives and commissions
- Benefits and insurance (partial or full)
- Prizes, trips or gifts
- Paid time off

A CRITICAL KPE ELEMENT

Individuals excel and achieve when they are driven to reach for more. Although a well-designed compensation plan is only one of the tools that is needed for Frontline success, it is one of the more critical and influential elements of the KPE for achieving peak potential.

The impact of an effective compensation plan when the other elements of the KPE are also in place, is exponential. Performance improvements increase your ability to compensate your team better. Then, you can hold your employees more accountable for performance because they have more to lose. When this is the case, *they perform.* Turnover becomes lower and you have less of a need to recruit. When you do, a limited "supply" of open positions allows you to be more selective.

Further, your current employees become a source of recruitment for you. When word spreads that you offer a great environment *and* great pay, potential employees start flooding in. As a result, turnover decreases while performance improves and generates more consistent results. We have seen and been involved in this process numerous times.

We will discuss this critical area further in chapter 6 and chapter 9, when we discuss compensation in greater detail and dig more deeply into implementation and effective sales management.

3. Communication

To understand the positive impact of communication in an organization, perhaps it is better to consider the negative impact that *the lack of it* can have on employees. Without adequate communication:

> "The worse the news, the more effort should go into communicating it."
>
> — Andrew S. Grove, Chairman, Intel Corporation

- The worst is always assumed
- A cynical rumor mill starts taking hold
- Management bashing ensues

A perception that management is "out of touch" often sets in, allowing for a "do what you can get away with" environment for many employees.

In his excellent book, *Less Is More,* Jason Jennings profiles the world's most productive and efficient companies. One is Nucor, a highly successful firm in one of America's most troubled industries: steel. Its CEO, Dan DiMicco, credits open communication as a key strategy in its success. "Forget about bureaucrats managing our communication," says DiMicco, "Everyone has the right to call me." And they do. DiMicco answers his own telephone and returns every call to every employee. "When someone calls me, everyone hears about it and they know the system works and management is accessible and responsive," he adds.

Many organizations pay little attention to internal communication and wrongfully assume that key information will

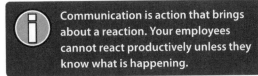

Communication is action that brings about a reaction. Your employees cannot react productively unless they know what is happening.

make its way through the office grapevine accurately by word of mouth. Communications that travels in such a way often gets twisted by gossip and gets distorted by preconceptions, additions and omissions. The inevitable result is confusion and employee discontent.

A POWERFUL TOOL

By speaking clearly and with one voice, you can use communication as a tool to keep the organization focused on what you feel is important, and to avoid the many tripwires associated with the rumor mill.

Some of the principal areas you should consider focusing on to improve communications are:

- **Company News:** Circulating news about big deals, key initiatives, executive promotions, company performance and product announcements

- **Product Knowledge:** Providing regular updates on and previews of your products and services in the marketplace

- **Customer Knowledge:** Communicating clear updates on key customers, marketplace trends and other information that will help your Frontline people be well-informed and knowledgeable to their customers

- **Best Practices:** Disseminating success stories, tips, effective sales techniques and other insights systematically so that all can benefit from them

- **Employee Recognition:** Identifying and publicly recognizing those employees who excel. It is extremely motivational for *all* employees to know that you are paying attention and value their success.

- **Employee Input and Suggestions:** This seemingly old-fashioned method can be very effective if management demonstrates that it values the input by acting upon useful employee suggestions.

COMMUNICATION CHANNELS

Internal communications should be considered a lifeblood activity of your business. It is best to create a few clear channels to deliver valuable information. Thanks to the flexibility of current information technology, there are many ways to do this. For example:

- Company newsletter—print or email
- Internal employee website/intranet-home page
- Communication bulletins
- Streaming media—online video and audio presentations

- Electronic meeting media—Webex, GoToMeeting or other electronic meeting vendors that allow you to engage even a widely decentralized workforce in communications as long as they have access to a computer
- Good old-fashioned one-on-one, as well as group meetings, always has and always will deliver the most impact.

> Effective internal communication is a critical and essential part of The Right Environment. It is the glue that holds your team together and a channel for straight talk and motivation throughout the organization.

4. Opportunities

In an industry that has traditionally been mired by many challenges and limited success, Enterprise Rent-A-Car has prevailed as one of the most profitable and arguably among the most successful organizations in the world. How have they done it? By *focusing on people*—and constantly communicating and providing incredible opportunities for those talented individuals who deserve them!

Opportunities serve as a means to spark the imagination of your managers and staff to visualize current and future success. The best businesses are driven by a culture of opportunity—a proactive and aggressive approach to looking for new ways to build the business and bring value to both internal and external customers.

When an "opportunity culture" is developed, the business gains and the most motivated "stars" find new ways to achieve and succeed.

> Nothing has more positive impact on employees than your unwavering belief in them and sincere concern for their growth and success.

CONSTANTLY COMMUNICATE THE POSSIBILITIES

Communicating possibilities is a powerful act. Consistently discussing company vision, mission, and potential opportunities, provides a vehicle for employees to achieve their hopes and dreams. Nothing can be more motivational.

Opportunity thinking can be grounded in the past, present, or future. For some companies, heritage is a source of inspiration. They may focus on how the motivated individual or group that founded the business took unique insight into the marketplace and built something new and valuable. For example:

- **The CEO of a major car rental brand started his career washing cars.**
- **The owner of a major Wendy's franchise began his career flipping burgers.**
- **The CEO of a major airline started his career as a ticket agent.**

Regardless of the size of your business, an opportunity-based culture is a key to getting the best performance out of your people. A large business often has multiple opportunities to allow for high performers to advance. A small-business owner can potentially satisfy star employees by making them partners in the growth of the business. They can utilize them to scale their own abilities and to open up new locations, expand the business in other verticals, and so on.

OPPORTUNITY CULTURE: NO PLACE FOR INSECURITY

Many executives are so isolated that they have no earthly idea of the potential of the human capital that resides within their own organizations! Others fear the high performer who may take their job. The latter is even more prevalent in larger corporations and in higher positions. This anxiety at the top creates a dysfunctional environment that limits your employees' growth, which in turn limits your company's potential. Face that challenge head-on. Do what Enterprise Rent-a-Car does; promote those who promote their people.

If you have your team members' best interests in mind, they will want to stay with you because of the opportunities you offer them. In the

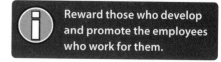

Reward those who develop and promote the employees who work for them.

rare case that their potential surpasses what you can offer, help them grow, and let them go. It is good for them, good for your business and more importantly, it is the right thing to do!

5. Support

Everyone in an organization needs and longs for the support of their leaders. But more often than not, Frontline managers are so engulfed in their daily operational issues and reports that they forget to focus on the real heart of what makes a business successful—their employees. Remember: *In many organizations most of the revenue that comes into the business is handled by the Frontline.*

Real support means spending time on the sales floor to ensure, among other things, that:

- You are addressing customer-service issues
- Your product delivery is smooth
- Your Frontline morale is high
- Staffing is adequate
- Coaching and feedback is effective
- Employee conflict is quickly resolved
- You are staying in touch with your customers

Supporting employees creates a positive environment that leads to stellar employee performance. Support your managers, have them support your employees, and take "the excuses" away to get them to do what really counts in business: selling and servicing.

➋ 6. Relationships

The United States is the hardest-working nation in the modern world. Americans generally work longer hours and take fewer vacations than most employees in other countries around the globe. With an average commute of over 45 minutes and a work week of 40-plus hours, most of us spend more waking hours at work and more time around our co-workers and boss than anywhere or anybody else. How horrible would it be if we had to work around people we did not like, trust, or enjoy being around?

Making the workplace a comfortable, even *desirable,* destination for employees is vital. Understanding personalities and how they mix, understanding who you bring into your culture and resolving conflict are essential to creating a positive work environment.

A NEW METRIC

The new workplace of today dictates that you measure great managers and leaders by the level of their team relationships. Having said that, good judgment must prevail. Being soft, easy, or fulfilling all of your employees' wishes may get some of them to like you, but it will not necessarily get them to respect you. That does not help you, them, or the organization that pays all of you.

Building relationships does not come by having beers after work. It comes through the implementation of much of what is in the KPE. Master it, build positive productive working relationships and watch the team you lead grow and prosper.

INSTILLING CONFIDENCE: NO BIGGER GIFT

Sit your team members down and look them in the eye. Instill confidence in them, train them, and build them up. In sales, more than other positions, they need it. Perpetual rejection is hard on one's self-image. Put them on

> "When I was a child my mother said to me, 'If you become a soldier, you'll be a general. If you become a monk, you'll end up as the Pope.' Instead I became a painter and wound up as Picasso."
>
> — Pablo Picasso

a pedestal, set high expectations, and help them to grow. Fortify this with strong relationships and watch them soar!

A great manager always possesses a positive relationship with his or her team. In fact, a measure of an outstanding manager is whether he or she *believes* in his or her team.

> **ⓘ** The power of what you can instill in people is limitless. Your belief in your team and what they can produce is perhaps the single biggest gift you can give them.

➲ 7. Input

Many owners and managers will say: "We have an open-door policy."

This phrase may be pretty common, although its application in many companies is spotty at best. Is your door really open? Or,

> Fostering dialogue starts at the top. Soliciting input is another way of learning what type, level and frequency of dialogue is present between the executives, managers and staff in your organization.

is it just cracked open? Or, worse—is it boarded up?

If your organization is not listening to its Frontline managers and employees, many consequences—all of them negative—will result:

- If you are not accessible, you are out of touch.
- If you are not in touch, your managers are out of touch.
- If your managers are out of touch, your people are not performing at their potential.
- If your people are not performing at their potential, your organization will not reach its potential.

Listen to what your Frontline is saying:

- What are their challenges?
- What are their perceived challenges?
- What are their needs?
- What are their perceived solutions?
- What solutions have they developed?

It is certainly true that the Frontline staff does not often perceive the "big picture" of the business the way most senior executives and managers do. But it is equally true that higher-ups are often insulated or isolated from the Frontline realities of the business. Frontline employees are often the first to see customer trends, product feedback, customer service issues, and other areas that are critical to the short- and long-term success of your operation.

It is very important to get this input in a timely fashion and it is essential that it be conveyed and received in an environment of respect and trust. If these valuable contributions are not treated as worthy of your time, they will soon dry up. Field input is also a tool that executives can use to get a clear vision of the day-to-day realities in their business-an intuitive view that standard reports and analysts cannot reveal.

CONDUCT AN EMPLOYEE SURVEY

A great way to solicit input is to simply conduct an employee survey. This can address a variety of topics and ideas that will help your organization reach its potential.

It is puzzling that many organizations will decide to wait to survey their employees because they have to "fix" a few things first, or, because they are not prepared to make some changes they know they need. The surveying process itself is a healthy exercise that shows that management cares about what is

happening in the business and about the employee experience as a whole.
Your employees may wait, but your customers and competitors will not.
Your employees may hang around, but if they are not happy, they will run
your customers off. Get input from your employees now. Be honest with them
and address the issues. You can then deal with the global matters in a "town
hall" type meeting, while addressing more sensitive individual ones on a
personal one-on-one basis.

Gallup research reveals the difference between relative and optimal
performance improvement.

*They had a happy and growing customer base all across New
Zealand, and were making good money. By all measures ASB Bank
Limited was a well-oiled profit machine and its parent company,
Commonwealth Bank of Australia, was elated with its performance.*

*The fact that things were going so well made CBA's request strangely
peculiar. Administer an environmental survey to your employees was
the directive. Although the ASB leadership didn't shy away from the
challenge, it did raise eyebrows as things were going very well.*

*What happened next changed the entire operating paradigm for
ASB. The results came in … and they were shocking. "We were absolutely
shattered when we learned we were in the bottom 25% of companies
surveyed," said Murray Beckman, ASB Bank's chief manager corporate
development. "We realized we had a lot of work to do."*

*And work they did. Knowing that improving the employee culture
would improve profits they attacked gaps in their environment, fiercely.
As a result, for four straight years, their culture scores improved and
their asset base bloomed by 20% annually, driving a cumulative
increase of over $7B NZ ($4.38B US) in a few short years.*

The most dramatic thing about this story is not the titanic increase in
assets. It is that these huge improvements were achieved by leaders who
thought they were already performing well. Their financial and service results
were strong, but compared to what or whom? If a seemingly strong company
can have these types of results, what kind of dramatic profit path can your
company cut?

Whatever input you get from your employees, the responses you make
will generally fall into three categories. Figure 4-3 contains a summary of
those responses with examples of how you might give feedback to employees
following a survey or other employee-input event.

The Three Essential Responses to Employee Surveys	
1. You are right	Thank you, we will fix it, improve it, and this is when we will do it.
Examples	• You are right! Adding a greeter makes sense. • Increasing the price of this item should improve our ticket average. • Excellent feedback on scheduling! Let's start that next month.
2. You are right, but	Thank you, but we cannot fix it or improve it, and this is why.
Examples	• You are right about upgrading our computers; however, this is not something we can afford at this time. Let's focus on increasing our ticket average. This can help increase our performance and help fund our computer upgrade, and maybe we can also have a nicer lunchroom for everyone to enjoy. A $3 per-ticket improvement is all we need. • I agree that you are deserving of a consideration for a promotion. However, I don't have a position in this location and you are not willing to move. Please be patient and keep up the good work. This will help us expand our business and create more management positions.
3. ARE YOU NUTS?	With all due respect, your request is unreasonable, and here's why.
Examples	• Giving everyone a 10% raise will erode all the company profit, and in turn, create instability in our business which ultimately jeopardizes your job security. • I am glad you want to move up and feel you deserve a promotion. However, your justification for performing poorly now because you are not challenged enough and are bored does not give me confidence to think you will perform strongly when you get a promotion and have more responsibility. • I am sorry I can't double your commission for that large contract. I am appreciative of your hard work in securing it. I am happy to pay you all the agreed-upon commission you deserve. Please remember all the hard work others have done in supporting you and the investment we continue to put in this company to create the vehicle that gives customers the confidence in our organization to purchase the type of contract you just sold.

Figure 4-3: The responses you might give to an employee survey will generally fall into three categories.

Great organizations and great leaders engage their people continually, understanding the multitude of benefits that come from doing so. More importantly, they grasp the grave consequences of *not* doing it.

You want all your employees to feel they can speak honestly to share their insight openly about your collective undertaking. Anything less means you are leaving money on the table, and preventing your organization from realizing its full potential.

➋ 8. Trust

If you don't buy the lines to the right, most other people won't either. I cannot think of anything that hurts productivity more than a group of people who do not trust the company they work for. It is really pretty basic: If they do not trust you, then they do not like you, and if they do not like you, then they will not work hard for you!

> Money cheerfully refunded!
> The check is in the mail!
> I only need five minutes of your time.
> Let's have lunch sometime
> This hurts me more than it hurts you.
> — Anonymous

WALKING THE WALK

Trust in a company is earned through the collective actions of its leaders. Your employees notice how upper management treats them. Small actions by higher-ups play a big part in forming the perceptions that employees make about the organization. One way to see how employees develop trust would be to read their reaction to the following series of questions.

Do the leaders in my company:

- Walk the talk?
- Take responsibility for failures?
- Treat everyone fairly and equally?
- Have their employees' best interests in mind?
- Take time to develop their team?
- Openly communicate the good and the bad?
- Seek to do the right thing every time?

A KPE Killer: The Trust Gap

If the answer to some or all of these questions is "no," you have a trust gap—and maybe a larger problem. Trust and credibility go hand-in-hand. If employees feel you are not playing straight with them or that management is making excuses, a fundamental element of company dialogue is broken, and employee cynicism sets in fast.

> "To be trusted is a greater compliment than being loved."
> — George McDonald

Want to see the impact of trust in an organization? Just look at SRC Holdings, a diversified company that roared back from near death to become one of the most successful companies on the planet. Jack Stack, its CEO, credits its revival and current success to the fact that he shares everything with his employees. Everyone in the company can read the P&L and balance sheets that are promptly posted in the employee cafeterias. All employees are entrusted with the financials of the business and attend meetings to review these statements.

> **Cynicism is the number-one motivational killer in any organization. It flows through the grapevine and the rumor mill, and pulls productivity and performance into the gutter.**

Creating an environment of trust is critical for creating happy employees that will take care of your customers and help your business thrive. It doesn't cost much to take the time to build trust throughout your organization. The alternative, however, will cost you plenty.

➲ Build It, and They Will Come to Stay

The Right Environment is the foundation of the KPE. The Right Environment is how the individual connects and becomes bonded to your organization, fostering a sense of belonging and an obligation to perform at a high level.

Implementing these eight elements does not have to take an enormous amount of additional effort. In fact, a cooperative and productive environment should eventually *lessen* your workload by getting more people to sell and serve your customers more effectively, ultimately generating more bottom-line profit.

> **ⓘ** World-class organizations don't just assume that their people are their most important assets. They know it. And they act on it.

World-class organizations don't randomly introducing "flavor of the day" tactics here and there to improve the environment. They don't just count on "people person" managers in some of their departments to do the job and they don't just react by applying band-aid type approaches through short-lived strategies.

What *do* world-class organizations do? They make creating a great environment part of their culture. It becomes part of what they do and how they exist. The Right Environment becomes part of how they conduct business, part of how they live, grow, and prosper. The Right Environment and all the good that comes from it becomes part of their make-up. It *embodies them.*

The Right Environment becomes their culture.

Great companies empower people, believe in them, and invest in their personal development and growth. It is impossible to have a great company with sustained profit and growth without a positive environment.

NO-BULL KNOW HOW!

Understand the following eight interdependent areas that are your keys to unleashing peak sales performance.

Development – Utilize the most effective options for you organization; from one-on-one training and coaching to professional education and certification, etc.

Compensation – This is a critical KPE element. In a sales position it has to be a prominent self-sustaining motivational tool.

Communication – Utilize the right channels for it and do it often. Your employees cannot react productively unless they know what is happening.

Opportunities – Develop a plan for it and communicate and encourage it.

Support – Support your managers; have them support your employees. Take "the excuses" away to get them to do what really counts in your business: servicing and selling your customers.

Relationships – Develop professional relationships that instill confidence in your employess and your belief in their capabilities.

Input – Input = engagement = performance. Your "open door" policy needs be "wide open."

Trust – Without it your potential will always be limited.

BANKING ON IT!

The Right Environment is a simple and powerful concept that very few companies pay attention to. The ROI that it brings is clear and unquestionable:

Engaged Employees = Happy Customers = Peak Potential

Great companies understand the power of a positive environment and they walk the talk when it comes to improving it. What is great about this advantage is that you are in control of making it happen day in and day out.

THE RIGHT FIT: SELECTING TOP PERFORMERS

Consider this: In sales positions, bad hires alone cost companies hundreds of thousands of dollars.

"I am convinced that nothing we do is more important than hiring and developing people. At the end of the day you bet on people, not on strategies."
— *Larry Bossidy, author of Execution: The Discipline of Getting Things Done*

- At Tremron, a Florida concrete paver manufacturer that primarily sells to installers, a bad hire can easily leave $1.5 million on the table annually when compared to a top producer.

- At the First Choice Call Center in London, where travel consultants sell $5,000 travel packages, a bad hire can easily leave over $1 million on the table annually.

- At Thrifty Car Rental in Los Angeles, a bad hire can leave $300,000 a year in highly profitable incremental revenue when compared to a top producer.

- At Bluegreen Corporation, a leading time-share broker, the impact of a bad hire is in the millions.

It's universal; from a pharmaceutical sales rep to a cart stand sales attendant at the mall, from a luxury real-estate salesperson to a full-service carwash ticket-writer, the impact of bad hires can range into the tens and hundreds of thousands of dollars, much of which is lost bottom-line profit.

In fact, a global research study conducted jointly by SHL, a leading firm in the area of people performance and the Future Foundation found that the hidden cost of selecting the wrong candidate for a position equals $105 billion annually in the United States alone!

This chapter explores the details and key concepts behind the Khoury Performance Equation's Right Fit element in addressing the caliber and quality of the people who are working on your Frontline. It shows how they fit within the sales culture you are creating, with guidance on valuing, sourcing, and selecting individuals who will be consistent top performers.

No Immunity

No company is immune from the profit-hemorrhaging impact of Frontline sales apathy and weakness.

A study commissioned by the U.S. Bureau of Labor and Statistics states that turnover for the modern Frontline-selling organization averages 23.4% per year, with the number rising to 34.7% in retail. It is not uncommon for companies in the transportation, automotive, and call-center industries to report annual turnover in the triple digits.

If you couple this "employee churn" expense with the negative impact of below-average sales production during a new hire's training period, the impact is crippling.

The solution to all this is very simple and straightforward. Get your recruitment right! Ensuring the right personnel fit is a critical part of boosting profits!

Sculpting the Team

The objective is to shape your team just like Michelangelo shaped the *David*. The most successful organizations in the

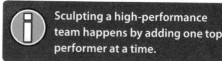

Sculpting a high-performance team happens by adding one top performer at a time.

world do this by thinking big, but acting locally. They get there by giving a sense of ownership to those who run their departments and their stores. It is these managers who have to *own* the recruitment process.

The Recruiting Psyche

One of the greatest inhibiting influences that keep organizations from becoming employment magnets for top sales performers is having the wrong "recruiting psyche."

Most companies recruit and hire people only when the need arises. They begin the process when they recognize a specific need—a visible position vacancy. When the organization is at full staff, management often comes under the illusion that the need to recruit is diminished. Nothing could be further from the truth. The fact is that the need to look for outstanding salespeople *always* exists.

◆ The Dreaded Transition Performance Gap

There are two types of vacancies, ones that are present and ones that are coming! You need to prepare for both because you never know when a future vacancy will become an immediate profit-draining hole.

Putting off the recruiting effort until the actual need arises is too late due to the *transition performance gap*. This is the acute revenue loss experienced by a company during the period between the sudden loss of an existing sales performer and the sourcing, hiring and training of their replacement.

You just never know when you will have to quickly find another star salesperson. Remember, even if you have an unbelievable culture and company, it usually is not a question of "if" some of your better performers are going to leave; it is a question of "when."

Therefore, be ready! Practicing the last-minute, "best available candidate" approach instead of the "top performer" method will cost your organization millions of dollars over time. Moving quickly to replace the sudden loss of a strong performer requires a proactive, multifaceted, and on-going recruitment strategy.

◆ Exceptional Producers: 15 Attributes

Here are the Top 15 Attributes you should look for when searching for your next superstar:

1. **Integrity:** Can you trust this candidate?
2. **Confidence:** Can he or she handle rejection?
3. **Ego:** Is he or she competitive? Does he or she want to win?
4. **Self-Motivation:** Is the candidate looking for more out of life? If so, what is he or she striving for?
5. **Positive Attitude:** Will he or she lift co-workers spirits, or will they dampen them?

6. **Enthusiasm:** Will the candidate bring energy to your workplace, or sap it?

7. **Communication Skills:** Can he or she express himself/herself clearly and professionally?

8. **Team Orientation:** Can the candidate set his or her self interest aside for the betterment of the organization when necessary?

9. **Strong Work Ethic:** Is he or she willing to do what it takes and put in the effort to succeed?

10. **Flexibility:** Can he or she handle change?

11. **Intelligence:** Does the candidate have the aptitude required?

12. **Sincerity:** Does he or she show a true caring for others?

13. **Humility:** Does the candidate show a willingness to learn?

14. **Empathy:** Does he or she care about the customer? Can they relate? Can they bond?

15. **Professionalism:** Does he or she represent your company in the best possible light?

That is a lot to seek. You may be thinking, "Only in la-la land would I find someone like that, and if I did, why would they want to work for *me?*"

Well, they would want to work for you because you have the employer elements people are drawn to and are driven by. This, in fact, is the aim of this entire book which includes all the interdependent strategies that you will learn to put in place. Implement them, and not only will strong producers "want" to work for you—they will be actively seeking you!

The SEE Factor

Forget about experience, age, background, what industry the candidate came from and how many degrees he or she has. The *SEE factor* (Figure 5-1) is primarily what you should be looking for. If they have these qualities, then many of the top 15 attributes outlined above can be taught and instilled in the top performer you invite to be part of your team.

Look for the SEE Factor:

Figure 5-1: Judge each Frontline candidate by the SEE factor.

SINCERITY

Despite popular belief, "nice guys" do not finish last. I don't believe it, I don't see it in businesses owners that I am friends with, and I haven't seen it in the top salespeople I have worked with over the years.

Bad guys may get ahead for a while, or get ahead more quickly, but they eventually end up crashing and burning. In the end, *nice guys* always finish first. In professional sales positions, it is the *nice guys* who are and always will be the *real* winners.

Effective selling is "relationship selling." It is selling something you believe in. It is selling with conviction and purpose. It is selling sincerely.

This quality flies in the face of any sales "tactic" that is deceptive, tricky, sleazy or tacky. *You need earnest people who care about the customer and understand that what they sell will enhance the customer's quality of life.*

> ⓘ Sincerity needs to be a non-negotiable attribute requirement for any new-hire candidate you are considering.

EMPATHY

Empathetic people relate well to most other people. They like to work with them and they love to help them. Frontline people with this quality can relate to your customer, build rapport quickly and find common ground. They make great first impressions and instantly get customers to like them. These people make customers want to buy from them!

Empathy does not mean that your salesperson "feels sorry" for the customer or "gives the store away." It does not mean that he or she is "sheepish" about asking for the sale or maximizing on it. As critical as it is, empathy alone can be a killer if it is not combined with personal confidence and a strong will to succeed.

EGO

Your team needs people with integrity: people whom you can trust and who will stay and grow with you. Your team needs folks who can relate to your customers and represent your organization in the best possible light. Your team also needs people with *strong egos.*

What do I mean by "ego"? The word ego can have a negative connotation, but let's face it: every human being has it and it can be used constructively. A "strong ego," as opposed to a false sense of superiority, can be defined by the following traits:

- It makes your team members want to be the best.
- It drives them to succeed day in and day out.
- It does not settle for mediocrity; it wants to maximize every educational, financial and growth opportunity that comes its way.
- It does not crumble as a result of customer rejection.
- It knows that if a customer refuses to buy, it does not mean that "I lost and they won."

In short, you are looking for team members whose ego is driven by these critical KPE elements:

- Being recognized
- Making the most money possible
- Being accountable for results

Like many impactful things, the *SEE Factor* does appear to have contradictory qualities. These are the qualities of a humble bully, a likeable but tough competitor, a nice guy that wants to finish first. Make no mistake, however; these are the qualities of a top performer—the qualities of your next superstar. They are not common, and not easy to find, but they *do* exist. The following sections will show you how to find them.

➋ The Right Fit

So how do you use the KPE's Right Fit element to transform the strength of your Frontline team? You do so by embracing three overriding actions that govern how well you bring in and retain top talent:

Valuing:

- Understanding the profound, strategic and direct impact your Frontline has on your net profits
- Understanding that the easiest performer to find and keep is the one who is already working for you (often unbeknownst to you)

Sourcing:

- Understanding that the larger pool you draw from, the better your odds of finding The Right Fit
- Understanding the need to execute an aggressive, and perpetually intense "full court press" in your search for strong applicants

Selecting:

- Understanding the additional time spent in getting to the best person will, in fact, save you time and make you more money
- Understanding the discipline required to stick to the interviewing model we will discuss

If managed well, this pool of activities will eventually reduce your workload by cutting turnover, improving morale, and increasing employee self-motivation—making your team much easier to manage. This aids you and your Frontline management team by giving you both the chance to lead from a higher level.

➷ Valuing Top Performers

Jim Collins, author of business-building power-book *Good to Great,* found there were 11 companies that outperformed the Dow by a factor of at least three over a 15-year period. Much to his and his researchers surprise, many of these companies did not come from high-tech, high-profile, cutting-edge or high-flying industries. *Good to Great* describes one of the key metrics each of these 11 companies shared.

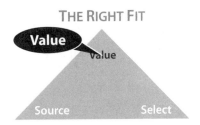

Collins states he expected to find that the first step in taking a company from good to great would be to set a new direction, a new vision and strategy for the company, and *then* get people committed and aligned behind that new direction. What he found instead was that the first step undertaken by the executives who pushed their transformations was to *first and foremost* get the right people "on the bus" (and the wrong people "off the bus"). Once that was accomplished, they then figured out the process of achieving greatness.

Universal Under-Appreciation

A point I make throughout this book is the widespread *lack of appreciation* we see from most companies toward their Frontline producers.

On the surface, and in most situations, the Frontline looks like an entry-level position, low on the prestige hierarchy in a business. The primary role of the Frontline in many companies is to first fulfill an order, and *then* to try and sell. For example, a car rental agent first fulfills a reservation and *then* tries to upgrade a customer to a more comfortable vehicle. A front desk clerk first processes the reservation *then* tries to upgrade the customer to a suite.

Even when a Frontline position is defined strictly as "sales" (such as an associate behind the fragrance counter at a department store), the perception by an organization's powers-that-be is that selling is an easy job. They think it's easy because the product or service being sold is fairly basic and they may feel "most customers know what they want."

> Understanding and appreciating the challenging nature of Frontline work is a critical fist step to enhancing the quality of each team member you invite into your organization

Walking the Walk

To truly understand the value on your Frontline, do yourself a favor: go out and do it yourself for a day. Is it really that easy to balance sales and service? Is it really that easy to keep a positive outlook after five consecutive rejections, three of which came from irate and disgruntled customers?

"Talk does not cook rice."
— Chinese proverb

The pressure to repeat this process 10, 20, or 100 times each shift can be exhausting, to say the least. Most decision makers in Frontline service and sales organizations never came from the Frontline and have never actually spent much meaningful time there. Those who have that experience usually have a completely different perspective and appreciation for what really goes on and what it really takes to be successful.

We don't hire consultants who have not been top performers in the field. They simply cannot relate as well, and if they cannot relate, they will not be as effective.

Having said that, I want to also state unequivocally that there are terrific managers who understand the Frontline position. There are many managers who appreciate the nuances and the involved and challenging nature of making it all work. They usually have a very open mind and a great deal of empathy. They usually also make outstanding leaders.

I would agree that the Frontline position is not an extremely complicated one; chances are your Frontline is not selling million-dollar banking software. However, I absolutely believe that executing sales well on a universal scale consistently requires a great understanding and appreciation of the Frontline. It also requires a good deal of organizational depth and maturity.

VALUING FROM A CUSTOMER'S PERSPECTIVE

Your customers mostly interact with the Frontline and generally do not deal with anyone else in your organization. Customers don't care if you have a highly educated and professional staff behind the scenes. They do care, however, that the people they are dealing with are engaged, caring, and professional.

Does what happens in the back office actually matter to your customer? Your upper management's MBAs and PhDs do not "connect" your customer to you. What does matter, ultimately, is the interaction your customers have with your Frontline because it is through them that your reputation is built or destroyed. Essentially, it all comes down to this:

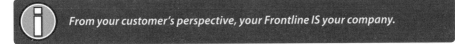

From your customer's perspective, your Frontline IS your company.

Do you truly understand that statement? Do your managers understand it? And, most importantly, do your managers' actions show it?

VALUING FROM A MANAGER'S PERSPECTIVE

Do your managers value the power and profit influence of the individuals in sales roles for your company, or do they resent them for what they perceive as "easy work" and in some cases "higher pay for top producers who earn bigger commission checks?" If the latter is the case, the result is usually a stark lack of support, resulting in salesperson demoralization, falling numbers, and grinding turnover.

- Understand and value the full impact of these team members, the "vanguard" of your organization.
- Forget about having your junior third-shift manager hire someone based only on a belief that the new employee will show up

to work and simply "handle" a position the manager desperately needs to fill!

- Identify the strongest people you have—this is your overriding objective. Then, make sure you keep them and add more high-potential talent!

- Go after *the* best to join *your* best!

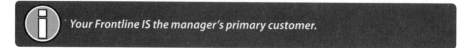

Your Frontline IS the manager's primary customer.

CALCULATE RELATIVE PROFIT POTENTIAL

I am cautious about being too repetitive when it comes to numbers, but quantifying the results are a huge part of what really drives this system and what fuels a Frontline Profit Machine. In fact almost every aspect of the KPE can be dollarized and the profit impact can be quantified in some manner.

> "However beautiful the strategy, you should occasionally look at the results."
> — Sir Winston Churchill

This exercise speaks to that impact:

1. Look at your top performers and compare their production to that of your below-average performers.

2. Take that difference and annualize it.

3. Now multiply this figure by the number of low-performing employees you have.

4. How does that revenue affect your margin and your bottom line?

Note: When figuring your net profit impact, be sure to consider the economies of scale traditionally associated with higher incremental revenue. As your sales revenue rises, your fixed expenses typically remain fixed, thereby dramatically increasing the net profit margin on the found money generated.

Following is one example from a familiar industry:

Karl's Rent-a-Center

- 10 salespeople
- Top two sell $2,000 per shift
- Bottom five average $1,200 per shift

- Difference of $800 per shift, per bottom
- Bottom five total *cost* per day = $4,000 ($800 X 5)
- Difference per year = $1,440,000 ($4,000 X 360)
- Margin on incremental sales= $576,000 ($1,440,000 x 40%)

Now analyze the implications of these figures:

- If your current net margin on new business were 10%, you would have to generate $10 in gross revenue to create $1 of net profit.
- In the preceding scenario, $576,000 dollars of net profit is being left on the table.
- Therefore, in order to generate the same financial impact of this sales improvement, you would have to generate $5,760,000 in new business annually, or add another 28,800 customers at $200 per ticket. ($576,000 x 10 = $5,760,000; $5,760,000 / $200 = 28,800 new customers)

Wow! Ask yourself what is easier: *To find over 28,000 new customers, or improve or replace the performance value of your weakest Frontline staff?*

The math is clear and the difference is staggering. These variances exist in the overwhelming majority of sales environments, regardless of product line, market or demographics.

Barry Leskin, the former chief learning officer for ChevronTexaco and chairman of the management and organization department at the USC's Marshall School of Business Research, has demonstrated that a company's top performers in mid-level to senior-level jobs are 50% more productive than their average-performing counterparts. With that kind of data, it's clear that your company's success depends on identifying, hiring and enabling as many of these top performers as possible. This is a critical key strategy in building a strong performance culture.

Doing this math is extremely important. After all, hiring and firing usually involves getting multiple levels of management on board by convincingly making your case.

Most managers know their lower-end producers are hurting the organization, but do they know how *intensely* these individuals are burning profits? Only when

> "I always arrive late at the office, but I make up for it by leaving early."
>
> — Charles Lamb, British essayist.

these losses are quantified consistently will most leaders take action. It is then when a full transformation in recruitment practices becomes a much easier sell.

JUST THE BEGINNING

Valuing the impact of your Frontline is a critical first step to making the changes necessary across multiple departments and decision makers to improve the quality of your sales and service team.

> **i** Know what attributes you need and want in your Frontline ambassadors. Then, make a personal commitment to get the right people on your team.

Sourcing Top Performers

Of all of the performance elements of the KPE, sourcing dynamic Frontline talent is universally recognized as the most difficult across most industry verticals. There are many authorities on this subject. Many have terrific strategies in concept, rooted in complicated approaches and sophisticated theory. At the end of the day, though, an approach with *practical applications* that produces results is all that really counts.

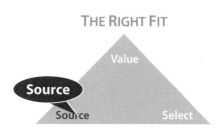

THE RIGHT FIT

With that being said, why is it increasingly difficult to find good people? Here are few of the negative influences that are contributing to North America's national crunch for effective manpower:

- **70 million baby boomers are beginning a mass exodus out of the labor market, creating cascading vacancies at all business levels.**

- **Newer, "Generation Y" employees who work fewer hours are slowly replacing the baby boomers' movement out of the workforce.**

- **Generation Y employee prospects do not respond as well to conventional hiring practices, but to more technically-oriented media. (See the Generation Y sections later in this chapter.)**

Recognizing these megatrends can make even the most confident recruiter a little anxious. The positive news, however, is that good people still want to work for good companies, and they will search for them.

FILL THAT BUCKET UP!

The goal of an effective recruiting program is to attract the highest number of candidates possible. This creates a large pool of applicants that you can then comb through and reduce to the superstars that you want to invite into your organization. Use the following recruitment processes as well as the "proactive recruitment approach" that we will discuss in Chapter 9 to create a large pool of applicants. Doing so eventually produces high-performing recruits who feel privileged to have landed the job, and who are itching to work and perform for your organization.

RECRUITING BY REFERRAL

Recruiting by referral through top performers is a highly efficient strategy for building your team. Why? Birds of a feather flock together. And in most cases, they are not looking at your ads because they are already employed! That is why referrals are your best bet for capturing them.

If a person is an outstanding producer, chances are that he or she hangs around people who are like-minded. Plus, if the terrific new hire already has a relationship with one of your best employees, it increases the likelihood that the current top performer will stick around for awhile. That person now sees the position not just as a financial outlet, but as a social one as well.

Having this ready-bullpen will minimize the damage from sudden and unforeseen manpower losses and the sub-

> Set a goal to have at least 20% of your prospect pipeline of desirable candidates made up of referrals.

sequent revenue erosion that accompanies it. What is of even higher value for the average owner is the security and peace of mind that comes with knowing you have potential top producers ready to join your team.

RECRUITING WITH ONLINE ADVERTISING

The Web has become a necessary part of today's successful recruiting arsenal. Whether you use an existing company website, a general massive job consolidator, a bulletin board company such as Craigslist or Monster.com, commit the resources necessary to gain some sort of online recruiting footprint.

Why? Younger applicants, especially those born into Generation Y (approximately from the years 1977 through 1994) are largely unreachable for companies without some sort of web-presence. In fact, a lack of online visibility can actually work as a forceful deterrent as potential employees may stereotype a difficult-to-find company as archaic and stuffy.

Furthermore, learning about companies online is perceived as significantly *easier and more enjoyable* than doing so offline. With an insatiable desire for perpetual "immediate gratification" caused by a world filled with a frenzy of instant messages, microwave meals and 24/7 cable-on-demand movies; youthful applicants do not just *like* the speed of online job-searching—they are practically *addicted* to it.

When faced with options of having to physically purchase and page through a newspaper, drive to several businesses, or sit and scan dozens of positions in a fraction of the time, there just isn't a comparison. Which would you rather do? Unlike driving around and getting caught in traffic, searching online (perhaps while listing to your favorite music playlist) can be fun, a treasure hunt with your company's job hopefully positioned under the big "X."

According to HR Management Online, recruiting practices are going through a technical evolution. We are rushing from the physical to the virtual world of talent sourcing. Going away are days of on-location advertising and temporary employment agencies. Today's game is played, and played fast in the online realm of bulletin boards, video resumes, and digital portfolios.

This metamorphosis isn't just impacting the job-source, but also the job-seeker. Becoming a hot industry of its own, online recruiting through companies such as Monster.com, Craigslist and HotJobs.com has moved from the back to the front of the line as a catch-all clearinghouse for millions of resumés and for nearly 70% of all job postings.

When it comes to recruiting in today's marketplace, if you are not online, you are not even in line.

RECRUITING USING MORE TRADITIONAL MEANS

Here are some traditional approaches to recruitment that can still be effective especially with you combine them with the interviewing process we will discuss later on:

- **Schools, colleges, universities, technical institutions: If you have flexibility in scheduling, people motivated enough to continue their education can do very well in a Frontline sales environment.**

- Military installations: Most military bases house a post-service job placement office where enlisted servicemen and servicewomen who are nearing their transfer to civilian life can find help in finding work. People with military honorable discharges have proven their ability to assume responsibility for their actions and to honor direction with respect and appropriate response.
- Special needs job placement organizations
- Our experience still shows that in many cases the Sunday paper still provides a huge punch.
- Industry trade magazines

CREATING A KILLER AD

An effective ad needs to be customized to the individual industry, marketplace and the recruitment needs at hand. This can often be a complex process, but here are some of the key messages that it should project:

A Challenge: We want applicants who have the SEE factor. That includes a healthy dose of ego! So the ad will have phrases such as:

- Only the best need apply
- Are you the best?
- Top performers only
- Are you up to the challenge?
- We are looking for the best to be around the best

The Offering: This includes such things as what top producers can make. I also like to break that down to hourly wage depending on the industry you are hiring for or the type of industries you are generally hiring from. Obviously, this can vary widely from company to company. Advertise what top producers can make, but don't exaggerate. And don't forget the non-monetary benefits your company may offer, such a as flexible work schedule, health and disability insurance and savings plans.

Here's an example of the key messages an ad might include:

- Free sales training seminar
- Top performers make up to $35 per hour; $70,000 per year

- No experience necessary—we will train you.
- Fast track to management
- Quality of life work schedule
- Additional benefits:
    » 401k
    » Health insurance
    » Tuition reimbursement

To Brand or Not to Brand

When we are involved, the decision of whether to customize the ad, or to brand the company for which we are recruiting, is collaborative; it is made with our clients and subject to their circumstances. We will recommend that we brand the company in the following cases:

- If the company we are recruiting for has a well-known name
- If the company already has a reputation as a great place to work and has a generous compensation plan
- If the company is located conveniently and will draw from the highest concentration of candidates in the city

Figure 5.3: Effective ads get you the numbers and the high-quality response you need.

Take a look at Figure 5-3. Here are some basic messages in this ad and why they work:

- A theme of urgency allows things to move rapidly and implies that this position will fill up quickly.

- Stating the average income lends credibility. Stating the top income draws in the superstars that otherwise may not consider working for your company.

- The ad is all about *them*. The benefits, the income, the paid training, quality of life schedule, fast track management opportunities, etc.

- The message is clear; the advertiser is looking for the best! The company wants to draw in the people that it believes are up to the standards it is seeking.

- The ad calls for face-to-face interviews. The advertiser wants to see how candidates are dressed and how they present themselves.

- Depending on the number of people a company is seeking, it may only ask that candidates call for an interview appointment, which will be booked in two-hour increments. This will further add to the sense of urgency and will allow potential new hires to see others applicants competing for the job.

THE FEAR FACTOR

I have been around Frontline organizations that are "afraid" of hiring aggressive salespeople. They feel that if they advertise that a person can make a significant amount of money, only sleazy salespeople will walk in the door.

Does the Nordstrom's team of salespeople, arguably the finest service-based retail sales force in the country, "push" their customers too hard?

What logic dictates that? And what lack of confidence do you have in your selection process that you can't weed out people who are truly overly aggressive? Higher sales will always improve service if it is done the right way with the right people.

You really have to ask yourself this important question: Are you going to be a professional service-based sales organization, or are you going to remain a meek and mediocre one? That's a decision you can only make!

CREATING A UNIQUE RECRUITING PROPOSITION (URP)

Most companies have some sort of sales process for their Frontline people to follow. Very few however, have one that helps managers sell the *merits* of working for their business.

Make your proactive recruiting efforts as effective as they can be by creating a *Unique Recruiting Proposition* (URP). Similar to the unique sales proposition used in other top-shelf sales organizations, this is a statement about who you are, and all of the reasons someone would want to work for you.

Unique Recruiting Proposition

Tim's Tire Stores—Sample Key Benefits:

- Second-generation, family-oriented business
- 37-year automotive industry veteran
- 6-time recipient of Best Automotive Business in Collier County
- 25-year member of our local community and Chamber of Commerce
- 12-year member of the local Lion's Club
- Faithful supporter to local:
  - » Police and sheriff's departments
  - » Fire departments
  - » Little League

Company provides:

- Team-oriented atmosphere, supportive management
- Professional training and development
- Safe and secure work environment
- An excellent opportunity to master Business 101 skills in a real-world setting
- Former team members include:
  - » 1 State Senator
  - » 1 State Representatives
  - » 22 College Graduates
  - » 7 New Business Owners

Figure 5-4: A Unique Recruiting Proposition will make your proactive recruiting efforts more effective.

So why would someone want to work for you? Can you answer that succinctly and with enthusiasm? What can they gain—not only in income and hard benefits—but also in valuable experience, prestige, owner's appreciation, a sense of belonging, skills development, and creative freedom?

Make Your URP Your Hiring Mantra

Once you articulate these added benefits, make sure you include a snapshot of them in your URP. Highlight some of these positive features in all of your recruitment ads and hiring materials. This reservoir of benefits will attract the people you want. Identify them and then use them to distinguish yourself from your competition.

Your URP should include the obvious—potential annual pay, medical/dental benefits, and also more subtle-but-equally-valuable benefits. These include (but are not limited to):

- Paid vacation or holiday time
- What top producers make per hour (including commission)
- Free training
- Free uniforms
- An opportunity to master interpersonal skills through daily customer interaction
- Educational opportunities in your industry context
- Fun and fast-paced work environment
- Team atmosphere
- Personal recognition ("employee of the month," monthly or quarterly "prizes" for top performers)

In today's world, recruitment is a two-way street. The following is worth repeating:

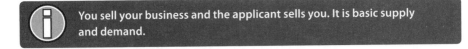

You sell your business and the applicant sells you. It is basic supply and demand.

This is pretty straightforward. The more you offer, the more demand you create for the positions that need to be filled. The more you offer the less turnover you will experience. Less turnover allows you to be more selective and to become the kind of company that *attracts* and *retains* top talent.

➡ Sourcing "Gen X" and "Gen Y" Candidates

As the next Generations, X and Y, take center stage in corporate America, learning how to recruit from these two demographic groups effectively will go from a business best practice luxury to a critical necessity. As such, it is paramount that you frame your organization appropriately to each respective demographic.

For the most part, sales teams over the next decade will be made up of Gen X and Gen Y personnel combinations; with each group having very distinct characteristics.

GENERATION X: MOVING FROM CYNICAL TO SERIOUS

Known as the "Lost" Generation for its small size (relative to its much larger Baby Boomer and Gen Y cousins), Gen X'ers are evolving into the new power-er brokers for the next decade. Born between the years of 1965 to 1976, Generation X has been labeled the "Cynical Generation" for its members' frequently pessimistic views on employment, longevity and employer-financed retirement.

Rising consumer prices, education costs, wild currency and home value fluctuations coupled with a shorter time to retirement has this group on high alert and hungry to produce for the right company ... while they still have time. An employer that provides immediate opportunities to grow a person's income relative to their specific effort (can you say a great sales commission plan?) is appealing to this group. *Focus on the present and the fact they can achieve what they want quickly!*

GENERATION Y: POTENTIAL DIAMONDS IN THE ROUGH

Generation Y is considered to be the more than 70 million Americans born between 1977 and 1994. This generation is slightly smaller than the Baby Boomer workforce, but twice the size of "Gen X." "Gen Y" is the most ethnically diverse generation to date.

Because of their over-indulgent parents and "hyper-consumer" habits, Gen Ys are also extremely motivated by incentives. Having a clearly defined bonus plan that pays well for top performance will attract them to your organization. Further, their ability to multitask through many different forms of communication and technologies allows them to adapt to high-pressure, hyper-dynamic working environments. Because they are the first generation to truly master the Internet as a research tool and information source, Gen Ys place a high value on product knowledge and concise information sound bytes.

STRESSING THE VALUE OF THEIR ROLE IN YOUR ORGANIZATION

Why is the role of each of these groups critical to the company's annual growth? Build this answer into your recruitment message.

Where Gen X'ers want to know where the money and opportunity is, Gen Ys want to understand why the company is approaching them. It is critical that you stress the importance of their "value" in the areas of company profit, customer experience and team dynamics. For both, characterizing their roles as professionals will make them appreciate their new position and motivate them to achieve their very best.

For example, a Frontline representative in a convenience store is not just a "cashier," but a sales associate involved with a $5 million-dollar-per-year site. He/she is also part of an ever-changing $554-billion-dollar-per-year industry.

RECRUITING STRATEGIES FOR SOURCING THE NEW GENERATIONS

Part of creating The Right Fit is a comprehensive recruitment plan. Consider all of the following points that will help attract valuable Gen X and Gen Y candidates.

- Design recruitment ads to depict a "community/network" image with team members of a diverse background.
- If applicable, have a top-performing representative profiled in the recruitment ads, providing a testimonial of why the company is a great choice.
- Place Gen X and Gen Y hot-button issues in the ads, such as opportunities to advance, flexible work schedule, fun and fast paced environment, diverse work group and performance-based incentive plans.
- Research your competitors' recruitment ads on popular websites. Look for the gaps in their ads and make a commitment to develop a more professional and more motivational ad.
- Develop a relationship with multiple professors at a local university and ask for five minutes of class time to conduct a brief presentation

on why your company has great opportunities for their students. Prior to the class presentations, develop and practice the message. Make sure you have prepared "leave-behind" materials.

- Post a career opportunity on Craig's List. Many of the postings there are free.

- If the applicant is not going to be hired, have a polite turn-down letter sent to him or her. Remember, Gen X'ers have a mature voice; Gen Ys have a powerful and well-connected one and each could one day become loyal customers.

- When communicating the next steps of the selection process, stress why the process may take five to seven business days and mirror their preferred communication styles via text, voice mail or email to set the next steps.

Selecting Top Performers

After reviewing the importance of valuing and sourcing potential top performers, you are now ready to actually select those you will hire.

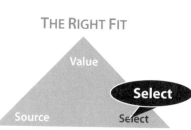

THE RIGHT FIT

You have powered-up your drawing capacity by showing how employment with your company is distinctly valuable, so you now want "the cream to rise to the top" by turning up the heat in your selection process. Two major objectives are achieved by making your hiring process difficult to pass:

- You eliminate those who were the wrong fit to begin with
- You create a feeling of tacit accomplishment for those who are able to "run the gauntlet" and earn the opportunity to join "your proud, your few"

We recommend a multifaceted approach that not only allows you to get to know your applicants surface strengths and weaknesses, but also the nuances that determine if someone has the right sales psyche to perform at a peak level.

This is coupled with a multitiered interview strategy that integrates the use of 25 behavioral drill-down questions. Last but not least, the system is rounded out with a hyper-objective, technical values analysis. The result is a person who is built for success in your Frontline Profit Machine. Let's take a look at each of these areas in greater detail.

A Bribe to Fire Yourself

In the world of online retailing you would not think of the practice of providing a "golden parachute" for a customer service representative, especially if that person was a salesperson in a contact center. But Zappos.com, an online shoe retailer, in 2008 offered a $2,000 bonus with no strings attached to anyone *who decided to quit* after their first week of training!

Zappos.com apparently did the math and decided it is cheaper to pay the wrong hire $2,000 to quit, rather than incur the expense of keeping that person on. When you think about this, it *does* make all the sense in the world. The $2,000 (an increase from the $100 the company offered when it first starting doing this), is a fraction of the real cost of holding on to a sub-par employee. The wrong fit kills sales, destroys service, and hurts your brand.

This kind of offer actually ensures that the majority of the employees who do stay on are even more invested in the company and its mission. This results in a "win" all around—for the customer, the employee and management.

A company like Zappos.com embodies the principles of a *Frontline Profit Machine.* Enlightened management in these companies fully understands that you can only engage your customers by engaging your employees, you cannot have happy customers without happy employees and you cannot "amaze" your customers without "amazing" your employees.

Do **The Right Environment, The Right Fit,** and The **Right Action** all pay off? For Zappos.com they certainly do. The "blow your mind" customer service stories and the incredible empowerment, belief, trust and confidence in the Frontline has helped increase the company's revenue 1,200%, from $70 million in sales in 2003 to nearly a $1 billion in 2008!

"THREE TO SEE" INTERVIEW APPROACH

Our suggestion is that you always conduct three interviews of each candidate before you select a new team member. This will allow you to confirm that the new candidate possesses the all-important SEE factor: real Sincerity, genuine Empathy, and a strong Ego that drives him or her to succeed.

Multiple interviews provide greater perspective. Each interviewer will interpret feedback through his or her prism and context. This blend of perceptions creates a three-dimensional view of the prospective employee's true nature.

Having three levels of screening also allows you to show the prospect that you are serious about finding the best person for the job. It also provides the applicant with an added sense of accomplishment if he or she are able to make it through.

A three-step selection process needs to be applied to all sales position applicants, regardless of the demographic source. Here is an example of a format that can be used:

Interview #1 The Screening Interview

Conducted by: Frontline Manager or Trainer

Time: 15 to 30 minutes

Purpose: To assess the applicant for fit and aptitude and to determine if a second interview is warranted

Interview #2 The In-Depth Behavioral Interview

Conducted by: Senior Branch/Location Manager or Performance Sales Manager

Time: Up to 90 minutes

Purpose: To determine if the applicant possesses the SEE factor as well as a majority of those Top 15 Attributes valued by the organization

Most companies want their employees to have these attributes, but many do not design a series of questions to discern whether or not their new-hires have them. With this in mind, a series of interview questions has been provided at the end of this section.

Design interview questions for stages one and two. Establish a "no comment" rule between the first and the second interview. After the second interview, the team can discuss the strengths and weaknesses of each candidate. Having this discipline will not place any pre-conceived notions in the second interviewer's mind.

Interview #3 The Final Interview

Conducted by: General Manager or Location Manager

Purpose: To ask questions about references and to give the final stamp of approval.

Time: 15 to 30 minutes

This session should be part final-screening and part vision-sharing. This ensures that the applicant understands how his or her sales successes will be of strategic importance to the company. It should conclude with the final offer along with compensation and training details, as well as a request for essential document completion.

POWER "TELL ME" QUESTIONS

Tell-me statements get you closer to understanding your applicant's performance potential. Create your own battery of questions and exercises from the following list, or use some of these in conjunction with your own. Just make sure the questions that help you identify the *SEE Factor* are addressed again and again throughout the series of interviews.

1. Tell me about yourself.
2. What do you know about us? What intrigues you about us? How did you prepare for this interview?
3. In your opinion, how would you rate your selling ability to total strangers and your ability to motivate them to buy now? Why do you feel this way? What makes you compelling?
4. If money and time were no object, what would you do tomorrow?
5. What were the last two books you read?
6. Describe your energy level. What is an average day for you?
7. How would your friends describe you? Business peers? Boss? Co-Workers?
8. What do you enjoy doing most?

9. How do you handle stress and pressure? Examples? What is important to keep in mind? How do you handle unwarranted disrespect from others?

10. What gets you really angry?

11. What motivates you? Why?

12. Why do you think you are so confident?

13. Tell me about the accomplishments you are proud of.

14. Which compensation structure would you prefer?
(This is not an offer, but a hypothetical question)
- $35,000 year guaranteed, or
- Only $20,000 guaranteed but with a real opportunity to make $65,000

15. What are your five best attributes?

16. What attributes do you think make a great salesperson?

17. Where do you think you will rank in the sales team you're joining? In one month? In three months? In one year?

18. How do you handle aggressive rejection?

19. How soon do you think we will see meaningful sales contributions from you?

20. Please define the following in your own words:
- Customer Service
- Sales
- Enthusiasm
- Upgrade

Another revealing exercise you can use to accompany the preceding questions is this simple assessment of an applicant's primary "wants from their employer." It immediately shows you what the individual's primary motivational drivers are and what will be required of you to elicit the very best production from them.

Ask the candidate to rate the following employer environmental elements in order of importance to you. (1=Critically important, 2=Marginally important, 3=Nice to have, but not critical)

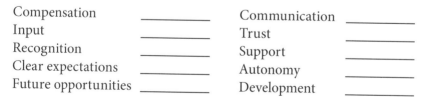

Compensation	_____	Communication	_____
Input	_____	Trust	_____
Recognition	_____	Support	_____
Clear expectations	_____	Autonomy	_____
Future opportunities	_____	Development	_____

After all interviews are completed, each of the interviewers should tabulate their scores and together select the right recruits.

USING ADDITIONAL TECHNICAL SCREENING

Have you ever hired "the perfect candidate," only to have to hide later as your colleagues whined, "Geez, who hired that guy?" We have all been there. Why does it happen? Why does someone who looks so strong and speaks so well in an interview eventually perform so terribly once hired? How can you be so far off, so often?

The answer is that those who are not good employees often become experts—not at their jobs—but only at getting jobs! They become professional interviewees. This is where the unemotional, objective eye of technical observation can be a huge help.

Once reserved only for Fortune 500 companies and high-level executive hires, sales organizations desiring the right attributes of employee confidence, sincerity, teachability, motivation and work ethic are increasingly seeking technological assistance. This allows you to screen out poor candidates from strong ones, and the best applicants from the marginal.

This also helps you to weave in additional technical tools to measure internal and external thought patterns that are difficult to pick up in behavioral interviews. Once a peak-performance psyche and a corresponding test result have been identified, you can then use them as future watermarks for all new potential applicants. Then you can begin to develop a hiring system that filters and approves salespeople who have the highest predisposition for peak sales performance.

There are numerous effective employment prescreening technologies and methodologies available in the marketplace. Choose what you feel best suits your type of business. Axiology is a system we have used with a high degree of success.

We have found Axiology to be "the cutting-edge technology" of subconscious value determination and ethics. Savvy sales organizations are able to morph this technology to see what makes their peak performers tick psychologically so they can replicate them on a macro scale through better recruiting and interviewing. The results are usually significant leaps in productivity.

Axiological assessments can be done for individual candidates, as well as to compare groups of high and low performers in order to isolate the unique performance characteristics within and between different sales initiatives.

➋ Doing What Is Necessary

Selling at the Frontline is not simple, but it is also not rocket science. Whatever the difficulty in your business, it certainly becomes much easier when you have the right blueprint to help develop and train your staff.

More than anything, selling at the Frontline requires a *positive attitude* and *an intense drive to succeed.* It requires individuals who handle pressure well, care for your customers, and demonstrate immense confidence. These attributes exist in people of all ages if you diligently search for them.

As we continue this journey through the KPE, you will begin to see how all of the elements begin to coalesce to form a powerful support structure capable of achieving the lofty goals we are targeting.

As you consider the difficulty in building a top-shelf sales team, remember that nothing that is supremely valuable comes easily. If it did, everyone would do it and there would be no competitive edge in it or a large return waiting for those who put in the effort.

You cannot just "do your best" and hope for the best. As outlined in this chapter *you must do what is necessary!*

KHOURY KEY TAKEAWAYS
CHAPTER 5

Sculpting your team by adding one strong performer at a time is the single most effective method to achieving a Frontline Profit Machine quickly and efficiently.

NO-BULL KNOW HOW!

✔ **Recruiting Psyche:** Get the right one in place that allows for a pipeline of candidates and that never passes up on a superstar whether you need them today or not.

✔ **Top 15 Attributes:** Look for all of them but do not hire anyone without the top three: the *SEE Factor*—Sincerity, Empathy, Ego.

Understand and implement the three elements of The Right Fit part of the Khoury Performance Equation:

Value:

✔ Great companies appreciate the bottom-line value of the Frontline. Most companies do not!

✔ From your customers' perspective, your Frontline *is* your company.

✔ From your managers' perspective, your Frontline *is* the customer.

Source:

✔ Identify the most effective channels of sourcing for your business.

✔ Identify a killer ad to include; urgency, financial upside, benefits that are all about them and a challenge for "only the best."

✔ Create a unique recruiting proposition.

Select:

✔ Adopt a three-stage interview process.

✔ Master the "tell me" questions.

✔ Adopt the right screening technology.

Understand and appreciate the make-up, psyche, and distinctly different recruiting approach for the biggest pool of candidates: the Gen X and Gen Y demographic.

BANKING ON IT!

✔ The Transition Performance Gap is a significant cost that you need to be aware of.

✔ Put the numbers to it and understand the impact of one good hire. Depending on the product or service you sell, that can vary from $25,000 of profit per year to $250,000 plus in profit per year.

THE RIGHT ACTION: ENABLING YOUR FRONTLINE PROFIT MACHINE

"Treat a man as he is, he will remain so. Treat a man the way he can be and ought to be, and he will become as he can be and should be."

— Goethe

Enabling top performers is the third and final piece of the Khoury Performance Equation. Even if you have built a positive environment and have infused some terrific talent into it, you will not capitalize on your revenue opportunities unless you unite them with *The Right Action.*

The Right Action in the Khoury Performance Equation is effective service-based sales execution. Without it, your mission goes nowhere.

This chapter covers specific methods of managing both the Frontline sales staff and the entire supporting organization to realize revenue opportunities left on the table. Combined with The Right Environment and The Right Fit, The Right Action will help you capitalize on the considerable remaining profit opportunities in your customer transactions.

So, where do you start? I have a very straightforward answer for you: Tell your team what you expect and then motivate them to do it! As simple as that action may seem, it needs to be part of a system so it can be applied and adjusted accordingly.

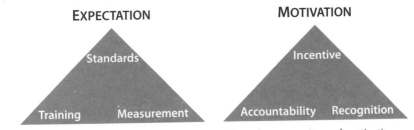

Figure 6-1: Enabling your top performers combines the right expectation and motivation

Here's how you can put this into practice.

➡ Setting Expectations

The challenge is often not with the expectation for the Frontline salespeople themselves; it is with the managers who should be leading them.

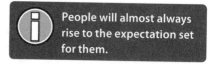

People will almost always rise to the expectation set for them.

Worry and anxiety often sets in on how to communicate and deal with new team expectations.

As they ponder this challenge, doubts start to emerge:

- How can I do this without my team thinking that what I am asking for is unfair?

- How can I do this and ask for performance that once was never considered achievable or possible?

- How can I do this without applying the type of undue pressure that may lead some people to give up and leave?

The answer is again part of the KPE blueprint, and part of the evolving plan to reach performance potential. The answers are clear and lie in focusing on these supporting actions:

- Creating standards
- Providing training
- Applying measurement

➡ Creating Standards

If you want anything done the right way, you need a standard for it.

Pretty basic, isn't it? So how often is this done in most companies of all sizes? Surprisingly, the answer is "very rarely." Even if these companies do have comprehensive standards, when

it comes to service-based selling, their policies are usually scattershot at best.

Your standards should encompass everything from your operation and training manuals, to your directives and your methods for doing business. These standards should include benchmarks, expected milestones, and performance goals that are set for every level at the Frontline.

It should include your objectives in areas such as service, key performer retention, productivity, image standards, and so forth. These standards need to demonstrate how you want things done. They need to be your best-practice methodology.

BEST PRACTICES FOR SERVICING AND SELLING

The KPE is applicable to any type of performance you want to achieve, but this chapter will focus on service-based selling.

What is your best practice when it comes to servicing and selling to your customers? If you do not know, how do you reasonably expect your people to greet your client guests, develop rapport with them, position your product effectively, overcome their objections and close sales?

Without clear expectations, you open yourself up for individuals to interpret your desired actions and you end up with loose results that nobody wants. Either you dictate what you define as good performance in an area, or it will be defined for you by your people—something you more than likely will not want or enjoy.

A COMMON WEAKNESS

Our experience shows that most training manuals are heavy on the technical aspects of a sale and very light on effective soft sales skills and techniques. This limited approach teaches people how to process a contract or write up a ticket. That alone does not really make you money. *What makes you money is selling consistently and doing so at a high level!*

The most common reason these employee guidebooks do not address successful sales behaviors is that, in most cases, they are developed by people who have little or no actual sales experience. Because they have "education" or "training" in their title, the assumption may be that they are the go-to person for creating a sales training solution.

> **Selling at peak levels while improving your long-term customer retention requires high level sales knowledge, experience and expertise. Your training materials need to reflect that.**

THE RIGHT ACTION SALES PROCESS

Each industry and the businesses within it should have its own standards. I will discuss best-practice sales and sales management in Chapters 7 and 9.

However, here are just a few samples of best practice questions you can use to benchmark and boost your profit potential at the Frontline.

- When do your salespeople greet the customer? How do they make the customer feel comfortable with them?
- If your business is conducted behind a counter, should you allow your salespeople to sit down? How do you break down physical barriers between them and your customers? What other effective body language standards should be taught?
- Should they ask for and use the customer's last name?
- What is the sales process flow? What are the standards for qualifying effectively? At what point do they offer the sale?
- How do you develop the winning strategy of top-down selling and what is the best way to get your Frontline to use it?
- How can you instill in them the hugely effective concept of discussing the product/service before the price?
- How do you ensure that employees on your Frontline always genuinely thank the customer, regardless of whether or not they buy anything from them?

THE RIGHT ACTION SALES MANAGEMENT

You cannot forget the managers. As I've already discussed throughout this book, your success is hinged to their daily practice of the KPE principles. With that in mind, here are some questions you should be asking about your Frontline managers.

- How is their daily game plan designed? Is it effective? What is the best-practice standard for its use?
- What is their standard for where they spend their time? Are they on the floor where it counts? When it counts?
- How do they set and communicate minimum standards of performance?
- Are they able to implement a performance-based scheduling approach, making sure that they have top producers at top locations, at the top times, handling the largest volume?
- What is the recruitment system they use?
- How are goals set? How often? Who does them? When are they done? How are your managers held accountable for achieving them?

⮎ Setting Up Effective Training

You have identified your company's best practice sales standards. You have developed your teaching materials. Once that is done, it will be time to put all of this into action—time to train your people.

Perfection is not attainable, but if we chase perfection we can catch excellence.

— Vince Lombardi

Here are the areas that you will need to focus on:

- **Company background and service/sales philosophy**
- **Technical proficiency, working with computers to complete/ execute the sales transaction**
- **The sales process**
- **Product knowledge development**
- **Common objections and rebuttals**
- **Personal motivation**
- **Personal image and professionalism**
- **General Frontline policies and procedures**

In the sales context, initial classroom training should include heavy emphasis on developing your team's product knowledge, facts on the specific features and benefits of products they will be asked to sell. In essence, the instructor should aim to turn his or her students into product-line experts: people to whom anyone can turn to for trusted product advice.

Training should also lay out the exact steps for executing a sale, from initializing contact with a customer completing the transaction, regardless of the outcome. I will share more of that in Chapter 7 when I discuss The Khoury Six-Step Service and Sales Process in much greater detail.

Pixar, the animated movie juggernaut, laid down a challenge directly to its 700 employees shortly after its birth in 1986: Make more films. Make them even faster. Make them even better. Desperately wanting to plant its own flag in the crowded movie-goer market, leadership knew it must elicit the creative passion of its employees if it was ever to make its mark. Hence, Pixar University was formed to develop and unlock its employees' potential for great filmmaking. It is focused on overall employee development rather than just a narrow, "company training-oriented niche." The university now has over 110 courses in its core curriculum, including those on painting, sculpting and creative writing. Every employee is encouraged to spend at least four hours per week on his or her own personal development.

The results have been nothing short of staggering, with Pixar hauling a veritable truckload of Hollywood hardware to their Emeryville, California headquarters over the past fifteen years, including twenty-four Academy Awards and nine Golden Globes.

THE WHY BEHIND THE HOW

A big part of effective sales training has to address the psychology of sales: why a person does or does not buy in a Frontline transaction. You must teach the nuances of interpersonal influence and persuasion. This step helps the Frontline believe in what they are selling. It helps them to connect further with the product, the company and the customer to whom they are selling the product or service.

ENTERTAIN AS YOU TRAIN

When designing the training presentation structure, keep in mind that these days people expect speakers to not only be educational, but to also be motivational and entertaining. Our on-demand, microwave-dinner-and-television-drenched culture will quickly lose interest in any presenter that does not make training interesting and interactive.

A huge part of the Frontline sales force is the "young millennials," those who have grown up in a digital world where media choices are ubiquitous and offered up constantly in small

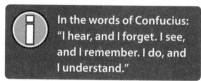

In the words of Confucius: "I hear, and I forget. I see, and I remember. I do, and I understand."

bites. That group more than any other easily gets bored with a one-way "talking head" type presentation. For these folks, the more interactive your presentation, the better.

Ensure that your developmental sessions are participatory, or you could further risk being flat and boring. You team members should look forward to your classes, not dread them.

It is best to use a combination of classroom and "on-the-job" training if you want truly dynamic sales results. Relying solely on PowerPoint slides and workbooks to provide the information and confidence required to be successful is impractical and largely ineffective.

Spice up your training sessions by:

- Integrating ice-breaking or team building exercises
- Adding role-playing segments
- Introducing contests
- Throwing in some quizzes and tests

Walk the Walk: Training Follow-Up

Following up Frontline seminars and workshops with real customer interaction is critical for building a salesperson's belief that the techniques shared in the educational sessions are not just conceptual, but practical as well. After the introductory training sessions are completed it is essential that what has been discussed is now demonstrated live and effectively on the Frontline.

You have to "walk the walk" and do it well to dispel the notion that leads people to think: "The training was nice, but it won't work with my customers."

Don't allow your managers to hide behind the countless phantom reasons or excuses they may come up with to be in the "back office." Minimize administrative needs and maximize team and employee face time. Clear standards need to dictate the amount of time managers and sales managers spend on the sales floor where it all happens.

Remember that running a smooth operation usually only puts your company at par. Spending time on the sales floor with your team and your customers is what makes you money.

Not an Easy Task

Building a peak performing team requires strong training and coaching skills. It also requires outstanding personal sales skills, superb counseling ability, motivational ability, patience, sincerity, and some statis-

> "A coach is someone who can give correction without causing resentment."
> — John Wooden

tical aptitude. It requires a thorough understanding of the influence of vocal tone and body language on customer purchasing psychology, as well as behavioral cue sensitivity.

That is a lot to ask from a single person or department, no matter how strong they are. But who said Frontline peak performance was easy? It isn't. That's why many companies don't achieve it, and that's why you have the chance to double your profits through it!

Quantifying Results with Measurement

Imagine attending an exciting football game. Then suddenly the power goes out. Without lights, a scoreboard, or an announcer's voice to guide you, it is impossible to keep up with what is happening. What is the score? Who has the momentum? Who is winning and who is losing? The energy is gone, the feeling is flat!

Many organizations function in the same way. They build and hype up their teams to climb the sales mountain, and many begin to climb ... but soon the team grows frustrated and bewildered, and the results dissipate. Why? They didn't provide enough light. They didn't have an effective scoreboard. The hype was fun, but ultimately, their team wanted to know if they were winning or losing. In order to give them the "scoreboard" they need and desire, you have to first have access to good measurement methods.

> "Keep looking below surface appearances. Don't shrink from doing so just because you might not like what you find."
>
> — Colin Powell

DESIGNING THE RIGHT REPORTS

Different companies, different products, and different services require different metrics—most of which may need to be reviewed, customized, and integrated in your reports. The key will be to identify the key metrics that are most critical to your bottom line, and then to produce reports that are simple, objective, and direct to reveal them.

Ineffective and inaccurate performance measurement in sales is all too common in many companies with Frontline sales opportunities. If the measurement is wrong, then the ground you are standing on is at best, shaky.

It is difficult to manage what you can't measure. Without accurate reports you cannot answer these critical questions.

KHOURY PERFORMANCE STORY

The Right Action for Peak Performance in Tough Times

It is fairly common knowledge that Bluegreen Resorts has among the best Frontline sales performance in the vacation ownership industry. The *Right Environment* makes it easier to attract and keep the *Right Fit* in an industry that is marred by high turnover. Above all, the biggest driver in Bluegreen's success is management's insistence on a strictly service-based and highly ethical sales approach that emphasizes a belief in the product and its value.

The challenge now was to transfer that culture into the customer service center that among other things activates reservations and handles cancellations. This challenge was made tougher as it had to be done in the 2008 real estate meltdown that dictated severe cost-cutting and a reduction in the number of staff. The management team did this by applying the *Right Action* elements to do more with a "whole lot" less.

EXPECTATION

Standards: Activating and saving reservations was a sales and revenue function that translated into bottom-line revenue and the *right standards* for how to do that were now clearly established.

Measurement: This new focus meant that the *right reports* needed to measure customer satisfaction and the show factor, an eventual win-win for the customer and Bluegreen.

Training: The reduction in staff forced managers to get closer to the Frontline, resulting in increased knowledge as well as more opportunity for motivation and implementation.

MOTIVATION

Recognition: A lean team now allowed managers to celebrate defined service and sales goals personally and more consistently.

Compensation: This team was now paid for results and brought into the results-oriented culture that existed throughout the organization.

Accountability: The reduction in staff expedited the opportunity to keep the right people in the right roles. The results were immediate and exponential.

The results spoke for themselves. Redefining the contact center's role also meant cutting out the menial and meaningless tasks. This combined with the right action elements above helped the center increase its revenue impact with *half the number of staff.*

1. Who really are your top performers? The highest total revenue seller could be costing you money, as shown in the example coming up.

2. Which are your best locations? The highest-selling ones could be leaving money on the table because the opportunities to sell are significantly higher.

FOUR BASIC MEASUREMENT CRITERIA

Sales data can come in many forms and depths. Regardless of your measurement system, you will want it to include these four attributes in designing your reports:

1. **Simplicity:** Reports should be easy to read and understand. They should also reflect the most important few numbers you are looking for.

2. **Accessibility:** Reports should be accessible by the Frontline so they can see their performance at anytime.

3. **Frequency:** Reports should be provided on a monthly, weekly, daily, and hourly basis to ensure perpetual focus.

4. **Relativity:** Reports should be pertinent to the task at hand and to the area of focus and responsibility you require from your Frontline.

If you don't already have one, you need to create a *flagship report* right now. If you do not have a point-of-sale system that generates these reports automatically, you may be able to create one in Microsoft Excel or a similar spreadsheet application, until you are able to automate.

THE RIGHT METRICS FOR THE RIGHT RESULTS

You can dissect numbers endlessly. Some of that can be useful. Most of it, however, will be a waste of time and an excuse for sales managers to act busy. When addressing measurement from a purely sales production perspective, it all comes down to a few metrics that drive critical performance:

1. Conversion

2. Yield

3. Total Sales

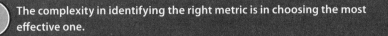

The complexity in identifying the right metric is in choosing the most effective one.

It may be best to illustrate this through examples of some key performance-driving metrics to ensure that you are measuring the right sales and profit indicators.

SALES CLOSING MEASUREMENTS

This measurement relates to situations where you have yet to acquire the customer.

Closed Sale Conversion

This is a percentage of closed sales relative to opportunities encountered.

- Formula: Closed sales made by the salesperson divided by the total number of customer opportunities to which that person has been exposed

This statistic helps you identify who on your sales team is helping you, and who is hurting you. Here are a couple of examples:

- A location encounters 4,000 customers a month and sells 800 of them. The location conversion percentage is therefore 20%. (800/4,000 = 20%)

- If Tom is running only 10% conversion on similar types of opportunities, and he encounters 500 customers, this indicates that he is leaving 50 sales "on the table" each month. (10% variance x 500 customers encountered)

- If the average sale is $500, then that equals $300,000 in lost revenue each year, relative to the location average ($500 sale average x 50 sales lost per month x 12 months). Assume this $300,000 would have translated into a profit margin of 20%. This seemingly innocent sales management slip-up just cost the company $60,000 in profit!

How many new customers must you find to generate another $60,000 in profit? If a company is also averaging about 20% margin on new business, it would have to generate $300,000 of additional revenue just to counter-balance the profit hemorrhaged by this one location-dragging salesperson.

Yield

This is a metric that relates to one of the following measures depending on the type of business you are in and/or the type of product or service you sell:

- Average revenue per transaction
- Average revenue per day
- Average revenue per customer

Here are a few examples:

- **Retail Store:** Jim sells $20,000 worth of warranties on 200 sales per month. His warranty sales yield is $100 per transaction ($20,000/200).

- **Movie Theater Concession:**
  » The stand sells $200,000 worth of popcorn and soda on 150,000 movie goers that year, producing a sales yield of $1.33 per moviegoer.

  » Julie sells $30,000 worth of popcorn and soda on 10,000 movie customers she serves that year for a sales yield of $3 per customer. Her yield is more than twice the average of the location.

If Julie's performance was duplicated by all the other attendants, the theater would have sold $450,000 of treats that year. If you were the theater owner, who would you want behind that counter?

UP-SELLING AND CROSS-SELLING MEASUREMENTS

In selling environments featuring multiple related products that range in price, the following calculations will give you the most effective measure of sales performance.

Incremental Yield

This is calculated by taking the "incremental revenue" above the base sales price and dividing it by the number of tickets, number of customers or length of transaction.

Example: *Contact center salesperson selling resort packages*

Here are examples of both total yield and incremental yield:

- **Total Yield:** Joe generates a total of $250,000 in room night revenue on 1,000 room nights a month. His total yield is $250 per night ($250,000/1,000).

- **Upgrade Yield:** Joe upgrades 10% of the customers into suites for another $150 per night. Assume the length of stay is the same per booking; that means Joes upgrade revenue is $15,000 (10% x 1000 room nights x $150). This leaves an incremental upgrade yield of $15 per night. ($15,000/1,000 nights).

- **Insurance Yield:** Joe then additionally sells $10,000 of trip insurance, producing an incremental insurance yield of $10 per night ($10,000 in upgrade revenue per 1,000 room nights = $10).

Percentage Penetration (Conversion)

This is another common calculation for measuring incremental sales. But this is not always an optimal bottom-line metric as the following example, using the same contact center shows:

- **Example:** Joe sold $25,000 of trip insurance on 1,000 nights with a penetration of 8%, resulting in a yield of $25.00 per room.

- **Example:** Matt sold $20,000 of trip insurance on the same 1,000 night volume resulting in an incremental yield of $20. He sold this amount of revenue with a penetration of 10% on trip insurance, a 2% higher conversion than Joe.

At first glance, this may not make sense. How can Matt have a higher penetration of sales but a lower incremental yield? The answer becomes very clear when you realize that Matt has the confidence to offer trip insurance only to the short-term customers, while Joe understands that the bigger opportunities exist with the long-stay customers. As a result, Joe tries even harder with them and in so doing, produces more revenue.

COMMON COSTLY MISTAKES IN REPORTS

Most organizations have too many reports. Worse yet, in most cases none of them are the right ones. Read the following examples and apply the takeaways to your business.

💀 Killer Mistake #1:

Reports measure conversion rates when they should measure average revenue yield.

Example: *Retail*

Many retail stores simply measure traffic and want you to "sell something to somebody." But it is not about how many items your salesperson sells; it is about how much revenue they generate. Let's look at the difference between these two selling strategies:

- Bob sold 40% of the customers at a ticket average of $10
- Debra sold 20% of the customers at a ticket average of $40

If Bob and Debra each had 100 customers, Debra would sell $800 to Bob's $400 in revenue. You don't need to be a rocket scientist to figure out that a report that measures sales conversion in this situation doesn't paint the whole picture.

💀 Killer Mistake #2:

Reports measure total revenue when they should measure conversion.

This may seem contradictory to what I have just discussed above, but it's almost as common!

Example: *Car Dealership*

John has seniority at the car dealership he has been working at for 20 years. His total sales are always among the highest every month. He rarely takes smoke breaks and his desk is in the best "real-estate" in the building.

Because his desk is at the front, he is able to see the customers come in, and if he is not with another customer, he usually is the first to grab most of the new arrivals. His total revenue is good because he deals with the highest number of customers. But does he do the best job possible of converting the highest percentage of customers?

Samantha, the newest salesperson with the worst-located desk and the slowest shift, doesn't have the highest revenue among the employees, but she has sold only four less cars for the month than John has. She has accomplished this even though she has been exposed to only 50% of John's chances.

In this case, the real measure of success is not just total sales; it is conversion on those valuable customers that finally walk-in, many of whom may eventually become customers for life.

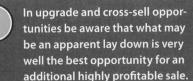

As customers become evermore valuable, it is critical that every attempt is made to maximize on every opportunity and not only measure sales in terms of total revenue.

CHURNING AND BURNING FOR LAYDOWNS

A key influence to learn and account for in many sales situations, especially Frontline selling, in which the customer comes to you, is the presence of *laydowns*.

A number of customers already know they want to either buy, upgrade, cross-buy, or any combination. These are easy conversions that require little or no sales effort. The num-

In upgrade and cross-sell opportunities be aware that what may be an apparent lay down is very well the best opportunity for an additional highly profitable sale.

ber of such customers in many Frontline companies can be anywhere from 5% to 30%. That reality has to be taken into account when you are measuring performance.

I was recently at a contact center and listened to the supposed "star" who booked $5 million a year in travel revenue. This lady was very authoritative, controlling, and fast. She was also churning through the calls. Yes, her revenue was great, but she also took twice as many calls as the average salesperson.

Her sales were the highest in the center, but her conversion was average. The company spent millions making that phone ring, but she churned and burned though potential customer after potential customer, searching for the easy sales. Revenue can easily look good with salespeople that "churn and burn" through the customers that come to and through your business.

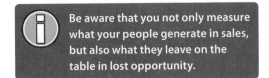

Be aware that you not only measure what your people generate in sales, but also what they leave on the table in lost opportunity.

AN ART AND A SCIENCE

Reports have to be customized to reflect the type of business you are in, the type of product or service you are selling, and what your goals and objectives are. In some cases you need a blend of metrics coupled with a prudent judgment call on how to best apply them for optimal revenue gains. Creating the right measurement criteria and the right reports is both an art and a science. It is critical that you understand both the psychology aspect of selling as well as basic financial math.

WHAT YOU DO WITH THE REPORTS IS WHAT COUNTS

Reports are great, but this information does you very little good if you don't understand how to use it to modify behavior both in service as well as sales.

For example, if a call-center salesperson has a low average "upgrade" price:

- The *typical* sales manager will tell him to get his numbers up.
- The *skilled* sales manager will tell him to focus on top-down selling.
- The *expert* sales manager will understand why he is not selling from the top down.

The expert sales manager will also focus on the core issue, and not the symptoms of it. In this case, there is probably some undercurrent of low confidence in the more expensive product and/or its current price.

Having the necessary measurements is only a part of your overall performance management system. You need to be able to make use of the information in order to be effective.

➋ The Final Piece of the KPE: Creating Motivation

This is the final piece of the Khoury Performance Equation. *The Right Environment* shows how to put a positive culture in place. *The Right Fit,* or recruitment part of the implementation formula ensures that the right people are in place. Your *expectations* have been set; best practice *standards* have been communicated, a *training* process has been established and you are able to *measure* your staff's progress clearly and easily.

Creating and sustaining motivation is the final step. This requires more than the occasional pep talk or contest. Motivation demands ongoing focus on three related human drivers and desires: compensation, recognition and accountability, as shown in Figure 6-2.

COMPENSATION:	**RECOGNITION:**	**ACCOUNTABILITY:**
The desire to make more money	The desire to be acknowledged	The desire to avoid negative consequences

Figure 6-2: Motivation demands an ongoing focus on compensation, recognition and accountability.

Understand these influences, and you will be able to tap into the performance-driving engine of your Frontline Profit Machine. Neglect them, and you will constantly be attempting to steer a parked car.

Determine how you can apply each of these motivational stimuli in your business to start getting *The Right Action* consistently.

🔁 Incentive: Impact Your Employees' Standard of Living

Most salespeople are highly motivated by money. There's no shame in this. In fact, if you don't have someone on your sales floor who wants to make more money, chances are you have the wrong person. If your individual Frontline employee has a minimum potential to  generate or influence over $50,000 in additional sales per year, and he or she doesn't absolutely count on their monthly commission plan, then you have the wrong plan.

HAVE TO HAVE VS. NICE TO HAVE

You want the type of monetary incentive that is more than the occasional nice-to-have paycheck; you need a *must-have* monetary incentive. Following the KPE, you will be employing the type of person who possesses the *SEE* factor: Sincerity, Empathy and a "strong" Ego. Your commission plan needs to allow that person to satisfy his or her ego and upgrade his or her standard of living.

Your incentive plan should provide this person with the opportunity to drive a better car, send his or her kids to better schools, take on a bigger house, or plan for a great vacation he or she once only dreamed of having. This employee now has no choice but to come in and produce!

This is why contests and gimmicky motivational schemes do not work over the long term. They can have a great impact over short spurts of time, but they won't change people's lives and they won't motivate them to consistently drive for the *big* results—and the *big* pay check.

MORE THAN SEMANTICS

The Merriam-Webster dictionary defines the word "bonus" as "money or an equivalent given in addition to an employee's usual compensation." I don't want to *give* more money! I want my employees to *earn* more money! I do not like to use "bonus" to define an incentive plan. I prefer "commission plan." Because "commission" is a well-known term for the percentage of what the salesperson brings in, it is more sales-oriented and more direct.

I know it may be just semantics, but I believe using the right words and phrases is an important action in building and shaping a sales culture.

Our clients' top salespeople often make twice the total wage of their competitors' salespeople in the same job, even though their base pay is often lower. Most of this extra income is coming through carefully constructed commission plans whereby both parties share in the upside. That is the way it should be in a thriving Frontline sales environment (even if some in the human resources department disagree!).

IT'S NOT WHAT YOU PAY, IT'S WHAT YOU KEEP

The key metric in compensating salespeople is not what you pay them. The key number is what sales revenue they generate and what you end up keeping.

I passionately believe in this! Prior to starting my consulting practice in 1993, I never had a job that paid me more than $30,000 a year in salary, even as regional sales manager. I did not seek it nor did I want it. I purposely negotiated a lower salary in exchange for a higher upside.

If a salesperson is good, if he or she is confident, that is what they will want. A very basic and telling interview question is, "would you rather have a guaranteed $18 per hour, or $12 per hour and an upside that would pay you $25 per hour?" The answer to that question should serve as a strong basis for your final decision.

PRACTICING WHAT WE PREACH

Today in our consulting practice, if we can baseline a client's sales performance accurately, we would rather work on a compensation option that has a heavy contingency component. In many cases we will even provide a 100% contingency option.

Once we perform our due diligence and determine what that upside is, we plan on a contingency option that would pay us up to 50% more than a straight fee option for the same forecasted results as we are taking on all the risk. We are open with our clients and we will share both options. We will then forecast the results as well as our compensation based on a how they choose to pay us.

Over time, and with our track record of results, we have had more and more customers opt for a fee option. That may give us added security, but it has also lowered our average per-day fee. We are in

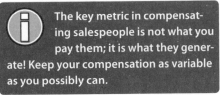

The key metric in compensating salespeople is not what you pay them; it is what they generate! Keep your compensation as variable as you possibly can.

the business of selling and achieving results. The client compensation plan we offer needs to reflect that. I use that plan to compensate our consultants and our salespeople. I strongly suggest you use these principles of upside commission with your salespeople and Frontline managers.

When working with this key principle, keep these fundamentals in mind:

- It is not what you pay; it is what you keep.
- You want salespeople that choose a lower base pay with a bigger upside.
- You want a plan that will impact people's day-to-day lives.

SOME BASIC PRINCIPLES FOR EFFECTIVE INCENTIVE PLANS

Here are some effective basic principles that we have applied to various incentive plans in a multitude of industries with a Frontline presence.

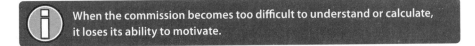

When the commission becomes too difficult to understand or calculate, it loses its ability to motivate.

Keep it Simple

No one commission plan can address every aspect of what you need done. As critical as the plan is, at the end of the day, it is your managers that need to manage your people. If a salesperson cannot calculate their current commission earnings in five minutes or less, your commission program is too complex.

Make it Easy to Measure

If you can't easily and precisely measure it, don't pay for it. Just paying someone off the cuff because you "feel" they are doing well is a recipe for disaster. Emotions are a notoriously poor indicator of true sales performance.

If you lack the technology to measure performance, establish an accurate manual report. Although not ideal, it is certainly better than not having a commission plan at all. In a short time, your increased sales should easily allow you to reinvest in the right reporting technology.

Tier it But Make it Attainable

The right plan needs to be realistic. As motivating as high goals can be, unreachable ones can demoralize your staff. And in some cases overzealous targets will create higher complaint ratios as your salespeople begin to push your customers past the point of no return. I am a big fan of a "tiered" sliding-scale approach to a commission plan. This essentially translates into more money for salespeople as they perform better on the opportunities that the company provides them.

Pay little or no incentive to the low performers. They are costing you money. Instead, take those funds and distribute them generously to those that produce. Take into account the *real* value of a producer. Understand that in many cases, top producers could move to another industry that will pay them more. Every business is different, but typically two to five tiers are the best way to go. You can start with zero payouts for weak performance that slides up to very generous payouts for the superstars.

Be Generous

Your top producers are worth it. Pay them well, or they will be producing for someone else! Calculate your ROI on every one of your Frontline staff. You will find in most cases that the ones that are paid the best are the ones that make your company the most profit.

Costco, now the nation's fourth largest retailer, has built a fiercely loyal workforce, with the lowest turnover rating in retail—five times lower than its largest competitor; Wal-Mart. Costco CEO Jim Sinegal has stated that the company pays its employees higher than average wages for its ambassadors—$17 an hour, or about 40% more than Sam's Club, in addition to an above-average benefits package.

*Sinegal knows that level of payroll cost may make Wall Street upset, but this maverick CEO has his eye on the long run. While Wall Street thinks in terms of quarters, he thinks in terms of tens of years. He knows that taking care of employees who produce keeps them happy and keeps them in the organization for the long run. The bottom line: Costco is hugely successful and very profitable. **Yes, they pay more but they keep more!***

Homework is Essential

When implementing or changing an incentive plan, you must take into account the current environmental situation in order to minimize panic and chaos. The things that need to be considered are:

- **Volume:** The more transaction volume handled per salesperson, the lower your percentage should generally be.

- **Salary:** The higher salary a person has, the lower the incentive opportunity should be. A more preferable situation is to have a lower guaranteed salary and a higher percentage payout of profit generated. Always try to keep the salary component less than 50% of a salesperson or manager's total compensation. Exceeding 50% in base pay results in some employees feeling that the small incentive payout isn't worth the extra effort needed to achieve it.

- **Sales Potential:** Payout percentages should remain near current levels if the company is near its potential. If the business has a lot of upside left, lower the percentage payout if results stay the same. You then trade that off for an upside that is higher as results move towards performance potential.

- **Starting Point:** If the company currently pays 1%, then there may be no need to jump to 10%. The Law of Incentive Relativity comes into play. This law states that all incentive changes need to be made in the context of the existing incentive plan.

I hope that these generalizations can provide some key takeaways. They may also provide a few "ahas" on what you are doing right, what you are doing wrong, or what you are not sure about!

Although I mentioned some variables that affect the design of a good plan, only a thorough *gap analysis* and discovery will reveal all the nuances of your industry, your product and the competitive field. All that information is critical to designing the most effective win-win, bottom-line-oriented incentive plan.

➋ Recognition: Play on Ego

Matt Eggen, my partner in our out-source call-center business uses the following pointed analogy: Anyone can take a sledgehammer and tear down a wall; however, to build something of value you need an architect, an engineer, 20-plus trades. The same

thing applies with people. Anyone can tear the people below them down, its unskilled labor. However building people up, identifying their strengths—that takes talent!

....

"A soldier will fight long and hard for a bit of colored ribbon."
— Napoleon Bonaparte

....

To some, recognition is a bigger motivator than money. Dale Carnegie, author of *How to Win Friends and Influence People,* wrote, "Be hearty in your approbation, lavish in your praise." The ego is a very powerful thing. Employment studies of Fortune 500 companies state the number one reason employees leave companies is that "they did not feel appreciated."

There are lots of ways and reasons to recognize your team members. Although we're focusing primarily on the sales arena, do not overlook the power of sharing your appreciation for good performances in these other areas as well:

- Service and customer care
- Overall professionalism
- Loyalty and tenure
- Effective recruiting of other key personnel
- Scheduling flexibility
- Doing the "small things"
- Attention to detail
- Good decision making

- Attendance and punctuality
- Image compliance
- Problem solving
- Initiative
- Policy compliance
- General productivity
- Sales or other procedural compliance

KEY RECOGNITION GUIDELINES

Recognition can take on many forms. It can be conveyed verbally, in writing (handwritten or in email format) and/or in public. Here are some other things to keep in mind the next time you show appreciation for a job well done:

- **Be specific.** If you want your appreciation to have any impact, instead of just telling someone, "good job," tell them specifically what was good about the job they did.

- **Convey positive feedback publicly when possible.** This accomplishes two things. It gives the recipient a tremendous sense of pride. Additionally, others who witness it will begin to hunger for the same recognition and start to improve their behavior.

- **Use varying forms or methods to show your satisfaction with a person's work.** One day you might just give someone a verbal "lift." The next time you can purchase lunch or a token gift for him or her. Mixing things up a bit will keep people on their toes and keep them from becoming desensitized to your feedback.

- **Verify that the recognition you are providing is legitimate and warranted.** Nothing is worse than calling together a sales huddle to recognize success that was unwarranted or undeserved.

You may have heard the story of the very successful salesperson talking about why he got along so well with his spouse. "Of course we get along great," he said. "We are both madly in love with the same person!"

The ego is a very powerful driver. Use it to challenge your Frontline performers to be their best so your organization can sell and function at its best.

➜ Accountability: The Fear Factor

Accountability, which adds a subtle fear of poor performance and subsequent consequences, gets people's attention and completes the triangle of motivation.

Recognition alone won't do it. Money alone is not enough of a driver. The plain truth is that most people are more motivated by fear than by any other outcome.

> Without doubt, accountability ranks among the most effective elements of the KPE. Without doubt, no KPE element is more overlooked and underutilized in organizations than accountability.

What good is providing your team with all the instruction and tools they need to be successful if you are not going to expect and require your staff to use them? The following analogy is very pointed:

> *"The weeds in your figurative pasture are the poor performers and negative employees who stifle the good attitudes and high performance of their fellow employees. If you're not pulling out your weeds, then it's likely their productive counterparts won't stick around to keep working with them. They'll choke out your best performers. Any environment where employees are not held accountable for their actions, whether they're positive or negative, can create a poor working environment. The greenest pastures are not filled with weeds."*
>
> *– Specialty Retail Report Online, Joanne Sujanski, Winter 2008*

ESTABLISH AND COMMUNICATE STANDARDS OF PERFORMANCE

In order to be effective in this area, you need to establish and clearly communicate your expectations and standards of performance. The fact is that most of the time, Frontline employees have customers coming to them. They are not hitting the road, making cold calls or networking to get sales opportunities; they are "receiving" the customer.

That potential customer costs money—a lot of money! While the company may *receive customers effortlessly,* it is paying for marketing, product development, infrastructure, buildings, financing, support staff, insurance, and more. The customer is a *produced opportunity* in which the company has invested greatly.

The profit that opportunity generates is very much affected by the actions of the leading service and sales personnel you have on the Frontline. It is therefore unacceptable for that Frontline employee to not enthusiastically greet the customer, qualify them, ask for the sale, overcome their objections and be responsive to their needs.

QUANTIFY THE SERVICE IMPACT

Studies show that a patron who leaves on the account of receiving poor service will tell up to 20 people! What does that translate to in revenue loss? Here is an example:

- Average revenue per customer: $200
- Average number of visits per customer per year: 5

- Average annual loss from customer dissatisfaction: $1,000
- Minimum number of years you want to be in business: 20
- Revenue erosion from losing this customer for life: $20,000
- Revenue erosion from losing this customer's circle of influence (20 people) for life: $400,000

That's $400,000 that can all be traced back to one dissatisfied customer. Who can afford this? So do the math, share it, and then do something about it.

CONTINUE TO QUANTIFY THE SALES IMPACT

In most sales environments the performance of the average salespeople is about 50% better than that of the bottom 20% performers. The top 20% performers are often 100% better than the bottom 20% performers. Apply the impact of this poor performing group to the numbers in your business.

- What does this revenue impact translate to in your catalogue sales contact center?
- How much revenue is lost in your apartment leasing office?
- How does this loss translate to the P&L for your clothing store?

Does this variance in performance make a difference in whether you have a good year or a bad year? How much does it increase profit? Does replacing the bottom 20% with a group that will perform at the level of the top 20% double your profit? For most companies it does!

KEEPING INTEGRITY IN THE EQUATION

In Frontline selling it is often easy to manipulate the system. It is also often easy to deceive and trick customers into spending money on things they don't even know they are buying.

> "Success without honor is an unseasoned dish; it will satisfy your hunger, but it won't taste good."
> — Joe Paterno

Expectations regarding integrity, above-board selling, clarity, transparency, and positive relationship-based selling need to be set early on. They need to be communicated constantly; they need to be reinforced and they need to be expected.

Recurrent training and floor time helps managers see if their students' sales are being closed with integrity, and not through any type of transactional manipulation. Once you've identified a cheater, or a manipulator, address the problem aggressively. It will send a message of zero tolerance and make management of future "bad apples" easier and less frequent.

MINIMUM ACCEPTABLE BEHAVIOR

> "It is not only what we do, but also what we do not do, for which we are accountable."
>
> — Moliere

You cannot allow poor sales and service performance to continue. This substandard effort jeopardizes the company's financial vitality and the rest of the team's job security.

In most cases, the cost of the "up," (the customer that comes in or calls in) can be quantified. Communicate that number to your staff and explain the enormous responsibility in servicing and selling that customer effectively. Let them know there will be consequences for not being diligent in helping the organization improve its revenues, and put a formal program in place to address this.

Contact centers spend millions to make the phone ring. Others spend millions on customer leads. Time Share and vacation ownership companies spend millions to get customers to tour their facilities. The cost of an up or a tour can be over $1,000 per couple. Can you imagine spending that type of money only to have apathetic, unenthusiastic, and passive salespeople receive those guests?

> It is unrealistic to expect your Frontline to achieve a sale or to provide a great service experience on every customer transaction, but it is also unacceptable for them not to try every time.

Once you have provided the tools, support, training and incentive structure needed to perform at a higher level, the responsibility then shifts to the Frontline. They have a "reciprocal obligation" to ensure their actions are consistent with your objectives.

UNDER-PERFORMERS: DO YOUR PART TO KNOW HOW MANY YOU REALLY HAVE

A business owner called me a few years back to say that he had heard me speak at a convention and he was now ready to use our services. He proceeded to also mention that he did not think anyone on his Frontline could sell. Should he fire them all and hire a new crop of salespeople before I got there, he asked?

My answer to him was that he really did not know who he had and what their capabilities are until he starts implementing the KPE. Working on The Right Environment and implementing The Right Action may bring out "superstars" you never know you had.

> "Most people are willing to change not because they see the light but because they feel the heat."
>
> — Unknown

We often get asked what percentage of a company's existing staff would actually be able to sell. Our general experience has shown that about 75% of the staff on a typical Frontline team—once given the proper training, tools, and support—usually stays on board and succeeds. Of course, that can vary greatly depending on the existing sales potential and the degree to which a sales culture has been established.

RESISTANCE: IT'S THE MANAGERS

The challenge of course is to hold that bottom 25% group accountable and to be prepared to move them out if they don't perform. The biggest obstacles to this are often not the salespeople themselves, but their managers, who may resist the task of terminating these weak players.

Here are some of the more common sentiments we hear:

- "But we have had a relationship with John for over seven years."
- "How can we do that? Jason is our most tenured salesperson."
- "What would the others think if we get rid of Natalie? They all love her."
- "Bill is a great guy and a great employee. He is just is not good at sales."
- "It won't be easy to find someone for the late shift."
- "It is just tough to fire someone for poor sales performance."

The bottom line is they are killing your bottom line. Take every step and procedure possible to support and help them out. If they don't improve and help themselves, help them further and let them go so they can find the kind of career in which they can really excel and grow.

Occasionally, you will have great employees that simply can't sell. In most cases you can find them another job within your organization. If you don't have one, help find them a job in the community or with a friend's company (as long as it is not a sales job). I will address the details of dealing with low performers further in Chapter 9.

⮎ Take Action!

Measure it, quantify it, share it and then do what most companies do not: *Do something about it!* Replacing poor performers with superstars can provide numbers that are staggering. Numbers that are *scary* good! Numbers that are exciting! Numbers that you can, and will, influence and control.

It is no coincidence that accountability is the last of the elements we discuss in the performance equation. It is placed there because once you have implemented and invested in everything else, it is now time to expect a return on that investment. So hold your team accountable! Most will get stronger and others will go away. Both will thank you over time.

KHOURY KEY TAKEAWAYS

CHAPTER 6

Tell your team what you expect and then motivate them to do it!

NO-BULL KNOW HOW!

The *Right Action* consists of the **Right** Expectations that must include:

➤ *The Right Standards*
- Identify best-practice service-based sales and sales management standards and processes.

➤ *The Right Measurement*
- Without accurate measurement reports and the correct metrics the entire performance equation is on shaky ground. Identify the right ones!

➤ *The Right Training*
- Effective seminars, workshops, and sales meetings as well as effective one-on-one coaching, all need to be developed.
- Trainers are not always the best sales managers. Identify the right ones. Then manage, motivate and hold them accountable by someone who understands sales and sales management.

The other part of The *Right Action* is the **Right** Motivation made up of these 3 elements that need to be applied in unison:

➤ *The Right Incentive*
- Commission plans need to be simple, attainable, and pay the top producers generously. The amount needs to become a "have to have" for producers, not "a nice to have."

➤ *The Right Recognition*
- Be generous in your praise for those who deserve recognition.
- Make it public and make it often.

➤ *The Right Accountability*
- No KPE element is more overlooked or more underutilized. Once all the elements of the KPE are in place, a minimum standard has to be set and it has to be "up" or "out" for weak performers.

BANKING ON IT!

Installing The Right Action portion of the KPE along with The Right Environment and The Right Fit completes all the pieces for a Frontline Profit Machine.

IMPLEMENTING YOUR PLAN FOR EXPLODING PROFITS

Long-Term

Mid-Term

Short-Term

CHAPTER 7

JUMP-STARTING THE SALES PROCESS

"The most distinguishing feature of winners is their intensity of purpose."

— *Alymer Letterman*

If you are determined to turn your team into a Frontline Profit Machine, this is "when the rubber meets the road." The interaction between your Frontline and your valued customer is the "moment" that counts. Everything we have discussed to this point has been designed to ensure that this "moment" is a winning one.

A successful transaction is defined as one that ends in a positive customer experience. It is one created by an effective Frontline presentation that has allowed your consumer to see and feel the very best your company has to offer. It is one where your product or service has met, or better yet, exceeded his or her wants, needs and expectations.

This chapter shows how to help ensure a successful transaction through three essential concepts that need to be reinforced daily to the Frontline:

What to keep in mind all the time:

The Guiding Principles

1. A Relationship-Focused Approach
2. Belief in Your Products, Prices and Sales Program
3. An Effective Delivery Process

What to bring to work every day:

The Selling Basics

1. The Right Attitude
2. Expert Product Knowledge
3. An Effective Presentation Style

What to offer the customer every time:

The Khoury Six-Step Selling Process

1. Greet and Build Rapport
2. Qualify
3. Present Product/Service
4. Overcome Objections
5. Be Prepared to Offer Other Services
6. Close Positively

In some sections of this chapter, I use a voice that speaks directly to the Frontline salesperson.

The Guiding Principles

The Khoury Guiding Principles (see Figure 7-1) are the heart and soul of selling. Your training manuals and "best practice" sales processes will have only limited success unless your Frontline staff rigorously follows them and actually applies them on a daily basis.

These are the pillars on which your sales foundation is built. Without them, the perception of selling becomes something you do *to the* customer instead of something you do *for the* customer.

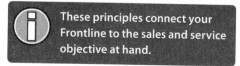
These principles connect your Frontline to the sales and service objective at hand.

Most importantly, these principles drive what is *the key* to successful selling: the consistent implementation of the sales process with *every* customer, *every* time.

THE KHOURY
GUIDING PRINCIPLES

RELATIONSHIP FOCUS   BELIEF   EFFECTIVE DELIVERY

Figure 7-1: You need to get buy-in on these principles to get your Frontline to sell effectively.

Follow a Relationship-Focused Approach

This principle addresses the importance of building an emotional connection with your customer, even if it is only a 30-second transaction. It says that when you

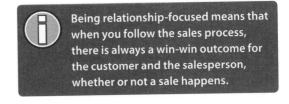

Being relationship-focused means that when you follow the sales process, there is always a win-win outcome for the customer and the salesperson, whether or not a sale happens.

sell your product or service, you have helped the customer meet his or her needs and wants.

If they buy, they will enjoy your product or service, and if they don't, you have done your job and you have better educated them on their options. The notion that when your customer buys, you have won and they have lost, is a poisonous mindset that will always limit your performance potential. The opposite situation implies that when the customer does not buy, that you have lost and they have won.

Being relationship-focused means we have the customers' best interest in mind every time. Does this mean we have to *sell* every customer every time? Absolutely not. But we don't know that unless we go through the sales process that allows us to qualify them and understand what their needs may be.

Believing and adopting this principle is critical to successful selling. In most cases, and in most businesses, more customers are going to say no than yes. It is a statistical certainty. In effect, when a salesperson possesses a strong win/lose psyche, they are actually setting themselves up to lose more often. This is because the "me versus you" mindset saps the customer's perceived sincerity of you, cripples your confidence and hurts your performance.

You should not get caught up in the number of "no" answers you receive. If everyone said yes all the time, your company wouldn't need a sales force. If you sell long enough, you will encounter situations in which you cannot help the customer. When they occur, have the good judgement to recognize the situation, instead of trying to force a bad transaction on the customer. That never pays ... for long.

No matter the outcome of the sales attempt, whether it is a "yes" or a "no," an overriding spirit of mutual goodwill must remain between you and your customer. Maintaining this positive attitude puts you in the best position to capitalize on the next, perhaps better opportunity.

Embrace the No!

Here is Michael Jordan's take on success. "I've missed more than 9,000 shots in my career. I've lost almost 300 games. Twenty-six times, I've been trusted to take the game winning shot and missed. I've failed over and over and over again in my life. And that is why I succeed."

What do these numbers have in common: 12,345; 4,195; 1,982?

They all represent the number of missed shots, missed attempts, or missed passes by the following athletes: Michael Jordan, Wayne Gretzky and Joe Montana. Did they enjoy rejection? Did they begin each of their all star seasons worrying about losses or missing shots? Obviously if you were a fan of these sports legends you know the answer is a resounding "No!"

Do you like to hear strong customer objections? Are you a big fan of the infamous "No, thanks"? I did not think so. The most effective salespeople truly understand that maximizing their time on the sales floor is not about selling to 100% of their customers *every* time, but simply offering to 100% of their customers *all* the time.

Although most Frontline teams will receive thousands of "nos" per year, they do not hear thousands of *different types* of "nos." In most cases negative responses from customers amount to between 8-10 different types of objections. Be prepared with detailed responses to boost your confidence and increase your sales.

If a customer says "No" to you—get over it! Don't take it personally. Channel your efforts and attention into an appropriate response and move on to your next customer!

Wayne Gretzky said "You miss 100% of the shots you never take!" If it was easy there would be no money or opportunity in it. Always remember that great performers will always be defined by their successes instead of their failures.

Ensure Belief in Your Products, Prices and Sales Program

> "A good leader inspires people to have confidence in the leader; a great leader inspires people to have confidence in themselves."
>
> — Unknown

In all of our experience, we have learned one indisputable truth: *The number-one attribute top salespeople have in abundance is confidence.* If your Frontline has it, they will be fearless in asking for fair value for your products and services. If they do not, you will always be battling uphill to close sales and struggling to capture prices you are happy with.

Confidence, in and of itself, can be elusive and fickle. *The greatest way to ensure your team demonstrates belief in the products/services they are selling, is to perpetually build Frontline belief in the value of those items and, just as importantly, belief in themselves as professional salespeople.*

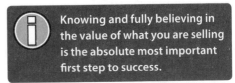 Knowing and fully believing in the value of what you are selling is the absolute most important first step to success.

Hands down, this is unquestionably the most important principle of all. Without belief, sales attempts become tentative, less frequent, and great service is almost impossible. Furthermore, when someone believes in what they are doing, they will do it autonomously and more consistently.

This principle is especially critical in a Frontline setting where you may have a very short period of time to sell the customer. If you don't believe in your product, your customer will see it and hear it. If you are scared to sell, they will become petrified to

> Warriors take chances. Like everyone else, they fear failing, but they refuse to let fear control them.
>
> — Ancient Samurai saying

buy. If you are shivering, they are shaking. In most selling situations you are selling yourself. *You* won't buy from someone that is jittery and doubtful, nor will your customers.

Confidence, on the other hand, creates a sense of safety and security for the buyer. They feel comfortable and affirmed in their thought process. They sense a sincere caring and competence from the professional representative. They feel the salesperson is truly there to help them and has their best interest in mind. People love to buy in situations like this and from people like this. Why? Because the customer does not "feel" like they are being sold or pressured. They are really being serviced and this is the right approach to successful selling.

Solving the Self-Projection Psyche

When you have someone who makes $25,000 a year representing your product or service, they often cannot relate to a $200 car rental upgrade, or a $5,000 Caribbean vacation. It is just not part of their world. None of us know what is in the customers wallet and nor we should we try. As such, it is management's job to explain and build the value of the sale on a continuous basis.

What does $150 mean to a couple who is spending the money to upgrade to a convertible so they can spend hours taking in a panoramic view of the city, enjoy the sunset and perfect their movie-star tans during their three day weekend getaway? This may be the only chance they ever have to drive a convertible. Do they want their pictures taken in sleek late model convertible or in front of the Ford Focus the travel agent booked for them? What is more important to them, the $150 that they are going to spend somewhere anyway, or the once-in-a-lifetime memory they will look back on forever?

> *Take an inbound vacation travel center. Although an average of $5,000 a booking may seem like a lot of money, most customers expect to pay that and more for a one-week, five-star luxury Caribbean vacation. Remember, they contacted you! When you look back on the most enjoyable moments of your life, vacations and time spent with family are among the top things you will remember. Focus on the great value you provide and the opportunity to make the customer's vacation memorable. People always remember the good times they had, and not the money they spent.*

When it comes to what your customers want to spend their money on, do yourself a favor and do not make up their minds for them. Instead, focus on the service and benefit you can give them.

If, after considering the full value of your products or services, you or your staff still think they are too expensive or not a great value for the right customers, then it may be time to find another job, or another brand or product line to represent all together.

Keep in mind, however, that many of the sales insecurities people possess have nothing to do with what they are selling, but are with who is doing the selling ... themselves. If your staff lacks confidence and belief, it will not matter what product they represent. People rise in life to the level of their self-image, and that's part of what is needed to help build a dynamic and thriving sales culture.

In a KPE culture, the Frontline are not clerks, they are not bodies and they are not order-takers. They are service and sales professionals. They need to know that, as well as the dynamic financial impact they have on your company. They need to know your expectations and take pride in the fact that you and your organizational have chosen them to be your ambassadors, and believe enough in them to invest in their success.

USE AN EFFECTIVE DELIVERY METHOD

Skilled salespeople are like old-school telephone operators. A person used to call in on one line, and the operator addressed the person's "need' by "physically" connecting his or her line to that of the person with whom they wanted to speak. The operator did not "sell" the person calling to the other person, the operator just connected them.

That is exactly what superior Frontline salespeople do. They effortlessly link your customer's needs to the benefits of your products and services. Once your Frontline understands this, so much of the pressure is removed. They can relax during transactions and more easily put their buying customers at ease.

Study your products and services and how they link to your customers.

- Know how they impact your customer's lives in the areas of building or providing comfort, convenience, prestige, fun, enjoyment, safety and security.
- Know how your offerings compare to that of your competitors.
- Know your strategic advantages, potential weaknesses and how to overcome comments about them.

Once your salespeople know what to say in every situation, they will become fearless, and a fearless salesperson is a formidable force on any sales team.

➡ The Selling Basics

The selling basics are just that, basic. They include common knowledge sales tenets like having the right attitude, knowing products and learning some important selling skills and strategies that allow a presentation to run smoothly. (See Figure 7-2.) Considering the high number of transactions in most Frontline situations, and the relatively short period of time available to make a sale, the effects of a "tight, fine-tuned sales presentation" are even that much more critical.

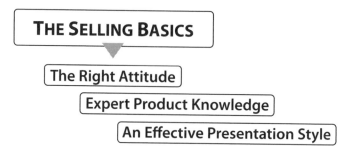

Figure 7-2: The selling basics include common-knowledge sales tenets that are critical to sales effectiveness.

The Right Attitude

I will trade someone with great talent and a bad attitude for someone with average talent, a great attitude, and an intense desire to succeed eight days a week. This does not mean that possessing an enthusiastic, can-do mindset all of the time is inevitably going to result in a sales bonanza. What it does do, though, is it always puts you in a better position to achieve greatness.

Think back to a time in your life when you were most positive, a time you felt energized, supremely confident and "in the zone." How were your mannerisms and speech different than they are right now? How was your physiology different? When you were "at your best," were you slouching and slurring or were you confident, enthusiastic, postured, and focused?

Is it possible to get back to that mental state, and then stay there perpetually? The most common response I get is, "Not if you work where I do!" What if someone offered you $100,000 to be more positive over the next six months? Could you do it? Usually, when I ask that question, people reply by saying, "I'm smiling already!" Your work situation is what you make it. The next time you are feeling unhappy about your working lot in life, consider this:

- The fact that you are reading this book means you have a significant success-building advantage over huge portions of the world's population, simply because you can read and have the freedom to do so

- The fact that after reading this book you have the freedom to jump in your car and go anywhere you want—without having to show security credentials—to work and to pursue greater dreams and goals if you so desire

- The fact that if you are a salesperson or are in a sales management capacity, you have the opportunity to exert additional effort and be paid for the fruits of your labor

- The fact that your employer pays you a base wage that you can use to offset personal expenses while you try to build a great lifestyle through your commission checks

- The fact that you, today, are most likely enjoying the benefits of sight, hearing, touch, smell and taste

- The fact that you most likely work in a comfortable environment shielded from the inclement weather

- The fact that you will take approximately 62,000 breaths today, when thousands upon thousands of people on their deathbeds over the next 24 hours, would give a whole lot to just to take a few more and live another day

If you were to calibrate your mind each morning by focusing on these positive areas of your life, before beginning your sales day, do you think it would help? Of course! You would be more pleasurable to be around, more earnest, more likable and exponentially more successful.

 People buy from people they like; one of your goals should always be to demonstrate an outstanding attitude or at least to try to actively improve it. In sales, you need to either be "up, or "getting up".

CREATING A POSITIVE ATMOSPHERE

Let me recount a specific situation I observed many years ago, that has always stood out in my mind.

A family of four arrived at a car rental counter in Orlando, all fitted with Mickey Mouse ears. It did not take a genius to figure out these guys were on a Disney vacation. This was in July around 4:00 PM when it usually showers for brief periods in the afternoon. So, here they are— Mickey ears on, super excited, and enthusiastic. Dad asks the agent behind the counter, "What is a good time of year to be here?" The agent looks back and quips, "March. That is when the weather is nice and cool." "Oh," comes a somber reply. "Well, does it always rain this time of year?" asks the dad, almost pleading for some hint of vacation hope. "Oh, yes, it always does this time of year," the agent answers, completely oblivious to this family's very special time.

Talk about popping that family's balloon! The agent could have made a more positive impact by telling the father his family looked stupid in mouse ears!

The right answer on what time of year is good to be there is *"right now"* because they are there right now! Every time of year has its pluses and minuses. The weather may not be as nice as it is in March, but it is also not as crowded and much easier to get on the rides at the amusement parks.

The response to *"Does it always rain?"* should have been, *"No, not all the time. However, when it does, it is only for a little while. It cools the weather down and makes it more pleasant in the evening."*

The issue here had nothing to do with the weather. It is indicative of the ambivalent or even negative mindset of a salesperson that inevitably always results in weaker sales. People spend money when they feel good. They spend money when they are motivated. They spend money when they are confident. The best salespeople are masterful at, in getting the customer into that mindset. It begins, though, with the sellers managing their own attitude.

CONTROLLING ATTITUDE

You may have noticed I am big fan of the word control as it surfaces in much of the sales process and throughout this book. I often see salespeople start the day with such promise only to quickly slip downward within the first hour.

Bob begins his shift and greets his first customer with great enthusiasm and hope for a promising sales day. His first customer declines the sale. The next customer steps up and says no to Bob as well. The third customer is very negative and grumbles about everything Bob says and does. The fourth customer is respectful, but nonetheless declines to buy anything ... and that is all she wrote! Tilt! Game over!

Bob is now "cooked," "done" and 'in the tank." Bob is demoralized and sees every customer, in his words, as "tight" or "cheap." Bob feels he has the worst luck because he "always" gets the worst customers. So now Bob, who started off the day with such promise, just can't get himself to be really nice to all these "cheapos who are wasting my time." In fact, so that they do not "one-up him," he may not even try to sell them anything! The wheels come off and another horrible sales day is now in the books.

What is amazing is the affect that four consecutive customers can have on Bob's attitude.

Who is controlling whom and what? I agree that not every customer is nice and certainly not every customer wants all of your products and services. Having said that, are you going to let a customer come into to your location, or call you over the phone and ruin your entire day? You are there five days a week, 50 weeks a year. They are there for five minutes! This is your domain, your house. Give it your best shot every time and if the customer says no, then let it be.

You cannot control your customers; you can only control yourself. Recognize you have only so much daily emotional energy and that you will drain it if you go through a heavy mood swing every time your customer accepts or rejects your offer. They are saying no to your offer, they are not rejecting you personally.

➋ Instilling Expert Product Knowledge

When people spend money, they want to know that they are making the right decision. Customers must see you as a resource, a confidante and a solution. Selling something because it is "nice and big" is usually not enough. Saying it is "really, really nice" or "really, really big" probably won't help either.

The problem is that sales statements like this don't evoke emotion and they can sound a little desperate. Give your customers descriptions of your products and services they can sink their teeth into. Whenever possible experience your product or service firsthand. Take initiative to learn it better and how to make it more emotionally appealing to your customers.

DISTINGUISHING FEATURES FROM BENEFITS

I may be one of the few people on earth who loves infomercials. I am just fascinated with how someone can spend 30 minutes building up a spot remover, an ab toner or a set of knives that all coincidently sell for under $20!

My favorite infomercial was popular in the early nineties, and you may recall it as well. It promoted the Miracle Mop.

I remember catching the ad one late winter night after an extended business dinner in Calgary. This advertisement was nothing less than a work of art. How they translated features of this mop into tangible customer benefits was incredible. The miracle mop helped clean your house more quickly so you could spend more time with your kids. This, in turn, effectively improved your relationship with them and helped make for a happier home. By the time you had seen the Miracle Mop commercial three or four times, you were convinced it would do the grocery shopping for you, drive your kids to school, drive you to work, and even give you a massage after your daily workout. It was indeed miraculous!

Kidding aside, the point is they were able to take a $19.95 everyday product, exceptionally distinguish it, build up its value, and sell the "living lights" out of it!

Think about how the Miracle Mop makers found that much benefit in a simple product that cleans dirty floors. Then ask how your Frontline can learn the features of your products and services better, and then match them to your customers needs in other emotionally fulfilling ways.

If it is done with passion, selling—an apartment that someone will *live* in, a family vacation that people will *remember,* a car detail that will *protect* a *prized* possession or a pair of stylish shoes that will make a person *feel* terrific—can become both noble and fun.

Features are simply what your product or service offers. *Benefits,* however, are how these features actually bring value to the customer. Obviously, the benefits to the customer can differ greatly based on their needs at the time. A larger flat-screen TV may have features like "picture in picture," but these are not customer benefits.

The value of this product attribute comes in the form of how they can make a customer "feel" better. In this case, a superior "picture in picture" feature will allow the customer to watch both his or her favorite teams making for a more enjoyable NFL Sunday afternoon.

> **ⓘ** Features, although important, do not sell because they do not evoke emotion. Benefits do. Further, the shorter the transaction, the more influenced it is by emotional decision making.

↻ Enhancing Presentation Style

How you say something, in many cases, has more impact than what you say. If someone approached you sincerely saying they liked your tie or scarf, you would accept the compliment and be immediately drawn to the person who gave it to you. Yet, imagine if the same person said the exact same words, but came running at you full speed flailing the arms wildly and screaming the words at you with red-faced intensity and bulging veins in their neck, *"I like your tie! I said, … "I … like … your … tie!"* You are probably going to respond a little differently right after you call for the authorities and ask them to bring a big net.

The style, manner, and approach that you use to deliver what you say in a sales transaction are also equally important. The following seven guidelines will help you further develop an effective and professional sales presentation.

1. **Use Voice Control.** Use variation. Lower your voice to draw someone in and increase your volume and enthusiasm when appropriate to emphasize your key selling points.

2. **Be Clear and Concise.** After you build rapport and qualify your customer, get right to it. Make a recommendation. If you have a great product you believe in, it will benefit the customer. Be direct, not shy. Shyness will cost you money. Be concise about each feature or benefit. Going on and on risks confusing and losing the customer. Confused customers say "no" by default as they struggle to keep up with what you are saying. Share only nuggets of information, a little at a time so you give the customer time to assimilate the information you have given. Lastly, speak in simple terms they can understand versus overly technical descriptions that will lose them.

3. **Make Sure You Have the Customer's Full Attention.** One of the secrets to success in Frontline selling is to come across as though you are not selling. Not having your customer's attention and having to repeat yourself gives the appearance that you are forcing the sales issue. This results in customer-perceived pressure which is the death knell for a Frontline sales team. Engage them in conversation to get their attention. Then, keep it short, sweet, impactful and to the point!

4. **Show Confidence.** Learn how to use your sales dialogue correctly, then, prepare and practice … prepare and practice. Refine your presentation, role-play objections and how to handle them again and again. Most sales situations have less than then ten primary objections that make up over 90% of customer responses. Master them. If you have to think about how to answer a customer objection in the middle of a transaction, you do not know your responses well enough yet to capture every sales opportunity in front of you. Combine mastery of these dialogues with a strong belief in what you are selling and you're on your way to big results.

5. **Do Not Oversell.** Look for the "yes" ... whether it is a nod, a whisper or a resounding "absolutely." Then, when you get it, ring it up and *move on!* At this point, do not rejoice, do not fall in love with your customer, and don't keep blabbing. Like a great football running back that simply hands the football over to the referee without fanfare after scoring a touchdown, act like you have been there before. You sold them something of great value. You both won—thank them and get them on their way so they can enjoy your product or service.

6. **Use Your Sales Tools Properly.** The purpose of a sales tool is to help you sell. The tool cannot make sales for you. I see far too many employees who are dependent on fancy sales devices, and who actually forget that people buy from people. Remember that you control the use of the sales tools. In many cases sales brochures are lying around and before you know it, the salesperson is now competing with the brochure for the customer's attention. Well-designed sales tools can be effective as long as you manage them, and not allow them to manage you.

7. **Use Positive Body Language.** This can be the subject of another book solely on this topic. A study conducted by UCLA states that 55% of the messages communicated in an interpersonal transaction come from body language. Another 38% come from vocal pitch, tone and inflection. This means a case could be made that 93% of all communication has *little* to do with the actual words we say! Here are just a few tips to get these influences to work for you, instead of against you:

   - *Minimize barriers.* Lean forward if there is a counter be-tween you and a customer. This communicates to them that you "are on their side."

   - *Maintain eye contact.* It is easier for customers to say "No" if you are not looking at them. Of course, the reverse is also true. A salesperson who does not make contact is easy to reject. Consider the difference in a saying no to a Girl Scout at your front door versus an unknown telemarketer. There is no comparison. Eye contact also allows you to read a cus-tomer's reactions and to react accordingly.

   - *Smile.* It relaxes you and the customer, and tells them you are likable and approachable.

- *Nod Your Head.* This creates a "yes environment." People by nature follow those that lead. A confident, valuable presentation combined with nodding your head puts the customer in a favorable "yes" mood. People do not like to make decisions. In many cases, people do not make decisions to buy. They only confirm decisions to buy that you make for them.

- *Avoid Negative Body Language.* Scratching your head, looking away, shaking, rocking, and speaking timidly, are all examples of weak body language that harms sales effectiveness and kills your numbers. Avoid it!

➋ The Khoury Six-Step Service and Sales Process

Most Frontline sales transactions (phone or face-to-face) are quite uncomplicated. The Herculean task is to get the Frontline to use your established sales process consistently, day in and day out.

This section on the six-step sales process (see Figure 7-3) will give you a good starting foundation for a sales process that your team can follow.

Although some of these guidelines may seem fairly basic, do not underestimate all that goes into establishing an effective customized sales presentation for your specific type of offering. A combination of world class "universal sales processes" combined with "best-practice" sales presentation techniques for your particular product or service needs to be identified and established.

Take all that and introduce it within the six-step sales process, and you now have a proven winning system that increases your team's confidence and produces positive results.

It is important not to mistake having a process for being rigid, stiff, robotic or fully scripted. Soft skills are critical in a sale. As an example reading a customer and knowing when to keep going or when to move on, is important to effective selling. It requires discernment, skill and experience. However, a starting point and a sales plan are needed to create a framework in which varying personalities can operate and duplicate consistent success.

Figure 7-3: The Khoury Six-Step Service and Sales Process

In culinary circles, the phrase "to reduce" means to boil unnecessary fluid out of a sauce, soup, or meal in order to strengthen the flavors in the remaining dish. After allowing a "reduction" to take place, the end result is much more savory and delicious. Over our decade and a half of work, we have seen (and tried) countless different ways to maximize Frontline sales while protecting and improving our clients' existing levels of customer care and retention. Some things have stuck, while others did not make the cut. Year after year, we have reduced and reduced these ideas, boiling them down to what we feel is the most effective method to sell on the Frontline.

The following steps briefly describe a few key elements in each area of the Frontline Service and Sales Process:

Step 1: Greet and Build Rapport

If a customer does not like you, he or she is not likely to want to buy from you. How well you manage the first five to fifteen seconds of a sales transaction determines if you will even be given an opportunity to sell.

CREATE A POSITIVE FIRST IMPRESSION

- Realize your domain is a stage. How you handle yourself and the customer you are with creates an impression for the next customer who is waiting.

- Smile, establish eye contact, and create a positive "yes, can do" environment.

- The more energy and enthusiasm you display, the more your customer will want to follow your lead. Make sure it is genuine. Why wouldn't it be? You work in a great place and you sell a great product. If you don't agree, find a place that is great and a product that you do believe in!

- Compliment your customer, but do so only if you are genuine and sincere. This often speaks volumes about the salespeople on your team. Some find something they like in virtually every customer. The salespeople who like and care for their customers are often very successful in selling. Others who can't find anything to like in anybody are the ones that usually struggle.

PRACTICE MIRRORING

- Find something in common with the customer you are with. It can be as simple as relating to an area they are from, what they like, what they are driving, wearing, doing, needing, looking for, etc. People like people they have something in common with. They identify with them. The customer does not perceive them as a salesperson, but as someone familiar who has similar values and interests. Remember, if they like you they will find every reason to buy from you. If they don't, they won't!

- Once you master the art of mirroring, you also can mirror body language. How do you feel when you go into a store and you are in a rush only to find that the salesperson is stuck at a snail's pace, oblivious to your need to move quickly. Frustrating isn't it? Now, think of how you feel when you want to have a leisurely meal at a restaurant and the server is rushing you. The ability to read and relate to a customer and to mirror them accordingly creates harmony that has an incredibly positive effect on sales.

- Mirroring speed and tone of voice over the phone is also hugely effective. If you have to repeat yourself frequently, you may be speaking too quickly. If your customer is constantly prodding and peppering you with quick, short, repetitive "uh-huhs," you may be speaking too slowly. Listen for it and then adjust your speed as needed.

- Mirroring is also reacting to a customer's needs and wants. You have to exercise good judgment in knowing when to keep going, when to stop or when to move on.

Step 2: Qualify the Customer

You cannot meet someone's needs without knowing what they are. Meeting customer needs takes you from selling to servicing. Some needs are obvious while others you have to learn. Here are some examples of cues that can make your sales efforts much easier:

OBSERVE EVERYTHING

- Mood
- Clothes, jewelry, taste
- Body language, facial expressions, tone of voice
- Other people in the party
- Who the decision maker is

PRACTICE ACTIVE LISTENING

- Listen for clues and information.
- Give your customer your undivided attention.
- Never interrupt.
- Confirm what you hear.

ASK QUESTIONS

- Ask questions conversationally, not confrontationally.
- Solicit specific answers. Begin with who, what, when, where, why and how.

Studying and practicing these three areas will help you master a basic service-based sales approach. It will help you meet your customers' needs, improve your company's profit and, most importantly, help you make more money. You will also learn a universal selling skill that you can use for a lifetime, regardless of where you go.

Step 3: Present Your Primary Product or Service

Always offer your best product or service that meets the customer's needs. An average salesperson who consistently asks for the sale every time will get better results than a great salesperson who asks for it only when they feel the customer wants to buy. Here are a few fundamentals in this area.

SELL ASSUMPTIVELY

You have a great product/service. Your price represents a great value. You have qualified your customer and now you know how they will benefit from your offering. What are you waiting for? It is time to take it up a notch. Expect a "yes" Don't ask the customer for the sale, tell them about it!

Stay away from these weak phrases:

"Do you want ..."

"Would you like ..."

"Is that okay/alright ..."

These statements put the customer in control. Remember, you are the expert. Replace them with the following assumptive winning phrases:

- **"What a lot of people like to do"—this is probably the most effective phrase in sales. Please make note that it does not say what most people do; it says what a lot of people do. "Most" means over 50%. If this is not the case, using the word "most" is being deceptive.**
- **"What I recommend"—a great line, especially when used in combination with the above phrase: "What a lot of people do and what I recommend is ..."**
- **"Based on what you are doing/need, here is a great way to go/do etc. ..."**
- **"Based on what you told me ..."**

FOCUS ON PRODUCT, NOT PRICE

This is perhaps the most common and most deadly mistake salespeople of all kinds make. If you lead with the price, that is what the customer will be fixated on and very little else. You can often rob yourself of the opportunity to present the value of your product or service.

Take control of the sales process. It is your business, your company, your service, and your domain. Don't let people come in, muddle up your presentation and throw you off your game. This happens when you allow a customer to get into a price discussion before discussing how the product they are interested in will help them.

Here is how you can prevent it:

- Build up your product up first.
- Get them excited. Selling effectively results in a transfer of feeling, a transfer in the excitement you have in a product to the customer.
- Show the value in terms of an emotional impact, not just money.
- Then, discuss the price confidently and in a very matter-of-fact manner. The relationship of value to price is critical. One product may be priced twice as high as another, but if the more expensive item will last three times longer, it is a better value. Communicate it!

UNDERSTAND QUALITY VS. QUANTITY

In most selling situations, especially in cross-selling and up-selling opportunities, trying desperately to get something from every customer is one sales strategy that many teach, but we disagree with it whole-heartedly. Expecting a "yes" on every transaction and having an anxious "this customer has to take something" psyche will grind your emotions and beat your sales energy to a pulp. No one can sustain that pulverizing outlook for long. It will wear you out mentally.

The idea is not to obsess about getting something from everyone. The idea is to find out what your customers need and want, and then to sell them the "biggest and best" you have that matches those desires.

If they don't need it or don't want it, it is time to move on. Let them go. If you try to push them, you are just going to create service complaints, which is bad for the customer, bad for you, and just plain bad business. Move on. Future chances to capitalize on easier and larger opportunities are just around the corner.

Give everyone your best shot then capitalize on those who are interested! It is easier to get one motivated customer to upgrade to the big suite for $200 a day than to get ten resistant customers to upgrade $20 each to the next level. This allows for better service as you don't have to push people into sales they really do not want. It also conserves your selling energy so you have reserves available for the big-ticket opportunities when they do come.

> In up-selling and cross-selling sales opportunities, it is easier to get more revenue dollars from a few customers you convert than it is to get a little from a majority of customers who may be resistant.

PRACTICE TOP-DOWN SELLING

This goes hand in hand with the previous point. Your most expensive products usually produce the highest levels of customer satisfaction. Additionally, offering the biggest and best you have does not mean you cannot drop down to the next level of service if the customer is open to it. On the contrary, it makes that offering sound that much more attractive.

Mastering top-down selling can be a real art. It helps you in these invaluable ways:

- It is a great compliment to the customer who may see himself or herself as worthy of the best.
- If you start at the top, the customer may just say yes.
- Everything sounds like a better value, after your most expensive offering.
- It allows you to gauge the customer's reaction to know if you should drop a little or all the way down so as not to lose them.

DO NOT PREJUDGE

Unfortunately, many salespeople have cocooned themselves with predispositions toward certain demographics. I hear these type of comments all the time; "this group over here never buys," or "these types of customers are cheap," and on and on.

Have you had someone who looked or sounded well-to-do, only to have their credit card be declined? If you have been in the sales business very long, it has undoubtedly happened to you. On the other hand, have you ever encountered someone who didn't look as if they had two cents to rub together, and they walked out with the most expensive thing you offer? And they paid for it with the "one payment plan"—cash!

Keep these thoughts in mind and never leave money on the table again.

- **Don't try to cherry-pick "buyers." When someone has a lot of money, he or she is not concerned about what others think. Their appearance may fool you, sometimes purposely.**
- **Assume everyone just inherited $1 million, and they want to spend it.**
- **If they take everything, treat them wonderfully. If they don't, treat them even better. The customers behind them are watching you.**

Step 4: Overcoming Objections

Why should you learn to overcome objections? Because you are going to get them!

Obviously, we all love those easy sales that come every now and then when the customer jumps all over our first offering. As nice as those "give me's" are, they are not as gratifying as the ones you have to work hard for by overcoming a customer's slew of objections.

When a customer responds with an objection, understand that they are not purposely trying to antagonize you; they simply have not been sold on the ability of the product or service to meet their needs and wants.

Here are a few guidelines to keep in mind that will help you better overcome common objections, and improve your closing ratio:

- **Don't try to win an argument. A man convinced against his will is still of the same opinion. Instead, focus on areas of common ground.**
- **Try to anticipate an objection and address it conversationally before it is raised.**
- **Match objections with appropriate responses. If a customer asks a question about how much additional time is required for you to process a sale, do not reply with something that references the additional price. That is not what they asked. If that is the issue, they will usually let you know!**
- **Speak in educational and conversational tones, like a counselor.**
- **Know your common objections! Practice and master them so you are never caught off guard.**
- **Be empathetic, be sincere and be humble, but also be prepared and confident.**

Step 5: Offer Other Services, or at Least Be Aware of Them

Always be aware of cross-selling opportunities. The easiest customer to sell an additional product to is your existing "buying" customer. In some cases, you may be responsible for selling only one product line. Even if this is the case, be knowledgeable about the other items your company offers. The customer will see you as an authority and will show more respect for your recommendations.

- Keep abreast of company product line changes, enhancements, and discontinuations.
- Focus on these sales at the end of the transaction, right before you wrap up. This will ensure that you do not sacrifice your big ticket item that comes earlier in the presentation for the small one at the end of it.
- Do not shy away from customers who have spent lots of money before reaching this step. The customers who have the greatest probability of saying yes are the ones who are already doing so.
- Remember that the customer is most likely going to buy these products somewhere anyway. So, why not buy them from you? It is the customer's most convenient option. They can make more money, they cannot make more time.

Step 6: Close Positively: Make the Last 15 to 30 Seconds Count

This is the "grand finale," so to speak. I am always puzzled why a server in a restaurant will do a great job throughout a meal, only to throw the bill on the table carelessly at the end and walk away.

Great customer experiences can only happen if your patrons are left with a positive lasting impression. Providing it reinforces the customer's confidence in your brand, and in turn, helps you build momentum you can carry into the next service or sales opportunity.

- Show gratitude whether your customer buys from you or not.
- In many instances you may need to explain all the charges clearly and ensure that there is no confusion over what they bought.
- Remind them of your name and that you are available to help them should they need anything. Avoid the phrase, "Call me if you have

any problems." It assumes they will and can scare the customer. Instead, replace it with, "If we can help you in any way, just..."
- Wish them a great experience using your product or service.
- Always wrap up with a great smile.

⊘ Master Your Trade

These six steps can take just a few short hours to learn, but years to master. Those who do master them will take a quantum leap in their sales abilities and career opportunities. As with any trade, a master salesperson spends years honing his or her skills. In the end, when that person can be certified as an expert, his or her long-term investment in these practices creates an efficiency that produces terrific results with seemingly little effort.

The good news is that you do not have to wait years to learn the secrets of effective Frontline selling. When it comes to learning how to peak perform in this environment, you have now been handed a proven and tested sales process. Master it!

The Khoury Performance Equation is set up for the purpose of mastering the most important few minutes in any business with a Frontline—the positive and professional service-based sales interaction between your team and your customers.

NO-BULL KNOW HOW!

The blueprint of the sales process is in the following three areas.

The Guiding Principle: What to keep in mind ALL THE TIME

- ✔ A relationship-focused approach. The customer's best interest needs to always come first.
- ✔ Confidence in your products, prices and sales program: Belief is *the* most critical attribute that needs to be built up.
- ✔ An effective delivery method: Master the process!

The Selling Basics: What to bring to work EVERY DAY

- ✔ The right attitude: Create a positive atmosphere and control your attitude.
- ✔ Expert product knowledge. Master the benefits and features of your products and services to build needs and to exude confidence and authority.
- ✔ An effective presentation style: Master and command the seven guidelines for an effective presentation.

The Khoury Six-Step Process. What to offer the customer EVERY TIME

- ✔ Greet and build rapport: Create a positive and sincere first impression.
- ✔ Qualify customers: Mastering this step turns "selling" into "servicing"
- ✔ Present your product or service: Focus on benefits and highlight value not price.
- ✔ Overcome objections: Know it, anticipate it, and be prepared for it.
- ✔ Be prepared to offer other services. This is the icing on the cake.
- ✔ Close positively, regardless of whether a customer buys or not.

BANKING ON IT!

The sales process alone will have limited effectiveness without consistent application. That will happen as you simultaneously develop **The Right Environment** and bring in **The Right Fit**. Mastering the methods above will create a succinct process that will transform the Frontline from *a cost center to a profit center*. Salespeople are not born—they are made. Apply this blueprint to make more of them for a win-win outcome for them, your customer and your organization.

CHAPTER 8

READY–SET–
LIFTOFF!

"To know the road ahead, ask those coming back."

— Chinese Proverb

Being fortunate enough to live in Orlando, less than an hour's drive from the Kennedy Space Center, I try to observe the space shuttle launch whenever possible. It absolutely amazes me to see and feel the power of the lift-off and to think that the astronauts on board will be looking down at us from outer space in a matter of minutes. Witnessing that was always a telling reminder to me of what can be accomplished with the right mix of talent, passion and dedicated leadership.

Not to sound too dramatic, but just as the space shuttle needs that explosive power to break through Earth's gravitational pull, you will need to reach "full power" as quickly as possible to catapult your team past the resistance to change, and on your way to becoming a Frontline Profit Machine.

So far we have examined the Khoury Performance Equation blueprint on how to build profit. I've discussed the effect of Frontline sales. I've outlined the actual sales process that should be employed. In this chapter it's time to look at your ultimate destination: understanding where you stand and then launching your journey to a winning Frontline culture.

However, like a space shuttle launch, you will need much planning, preparation, and determined leadership to propel you to "break through" and get you on your way to reaching your goal.

Here are a few key points to keep in mind when you are getting ready for "lift off":

- **It's all in the implementation stage.** In sales "culture building," many companies fail when they actually move to the execution phase. Much of this breakdown can be attributed to a *lack of understanding and confidence in the potential net profit impact of your team. Know and* *believe* that a superior Frontline can transform your bottom line. This will provide a more supportive structure for the KPE elements.

- **The KPE is an interdependent model.** All of the elements of each segment of the plan must be in place for it to function. A strong incentive plan combined with poor training and ineffective measurement will not work. If you can have all the elements of the "Right Action" in place except accountability, then you will fail.

- **Improvement is okay, but peak potential is want you really want.** You, your employees and your customers deserve the absolute best. You deserve the benefits that come along with elevating your organization from mediocrity to industry leadership. Do not accept marginal improvement results; go for peak performance.

- **The KPE needs to be implemented across all management levels.** This is perhaps a bigger challenge in larger companies. The same positive environment you create for the Frontline has to be created for managers. You also need to provide them with incentive opportunity, recognize them for performance and hold them accountable for a lack of it. You need to put effective "best practice standards" in place for them as well, along with the right training and an effective performance measurement methodology.

The task at hand becomes exponentially easier if you grasp the rationality and basic human nature that inspires and drives the elements of the KPE. This understanding is your critical prerequisite for success. Now that you are armed with it, lets get this journey started.

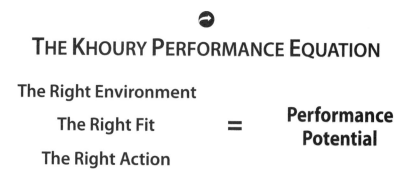

THE KHOURY PERFORMANCE EQUATION

The Right Environment

The Right Fit   =   **Performance Potential**

The Right Action

Figure 8.1. The Khoury Performance Equation unleashes performance potential.

⮕ Getting Started: The Right Plan

Your process for effectively launching The Right Plan can be summarized in seven steps, as shown in Figure 8-2.

Seven Steps to LAUNCHING THE RIGHT PLAN

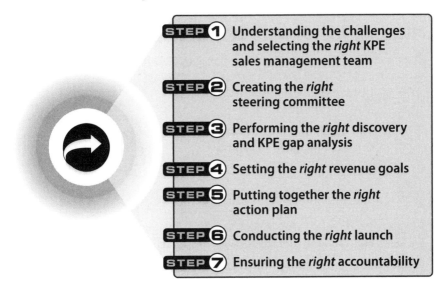

STEP ① Understanding the challenges and selecting the *right* KPE sales management team

STEP ② Creating the *right* steering committee

STEP ③ Performing the *right* discovery and KPE gap analysis

STEP ④ Setting the *right* revenue goals

STEP ⑤ Putting together the *right* action plan

STEP ⑥ Conducting the *right* launch

STEP ⑦ Ensuring the *right* accountability

Figure 8-2: Your process for effectively launching The Right Plan can be summarized in seven steps.

Prioritize these steps in terms of short-term, mid-term and long-term goals, all corresponding to key KPE elements, as shown in Figure 8-3. This prioritization is critical to assure speedy implementation and the fastest impact on your business (see Figure 8-4).

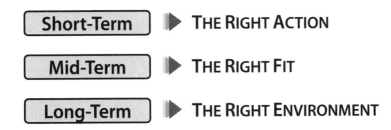

Short-Term ▶ THE RIGHT ACTION

Mid-Term ▶ THE RIGHT FIT

Long-Term ▶ THE RIGHT ENVIRONMENT

Figure 8-3. Your short-term, mid-term, and long-term goals correspond to key KPE elements.

We often see what we term as *performance emergencies* in Frontline companies. Many organizations lack the basic elements that are within The Right Action portion of the KPE. It is a performance emergency, for example, if reporting is lacking or inaccurate. It is difficult to measure performance if there is no real defined sales process, or a weak training program. It is tough to motivate people with a non-existent or poorly constructed commission plan.

THE HARD COST OF SOFT COMMITMENT

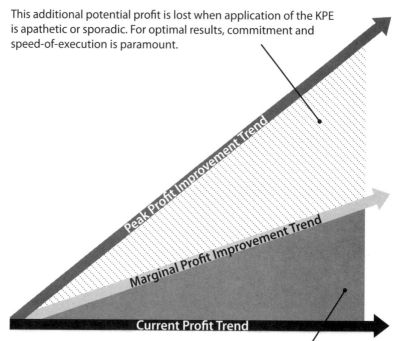

This additional potential profit is lost when application of the KPE is apathetic or sporadic. For optimal results, commitment and speed-of-execution is paramount.

Peak Profit Improvement Trend

Marginal Profit Improvement Trend

Current Profit Trend

Due to its power to transform performance, even applying pieces of the KPE will produce some profit improvement.

Figure 8-4: Speedy implementation of KPE principles is critical to assuring the fastest impact on your business.

The elements that belong in The Right Action need to be addressed first. The next steps are to address the recruitment for The Right Fit. Finally, and although The Right Environment needs to be looked at from the start, making changes in some of those elements does take more time as it requires more buy-in and more involvement from the top.

I certainly am not advocating that you don't try to go after all three areas at the same time. However you do need to start somewhere and this is the most optimal way to do it.

STEP ①

• Selecting the Right Sales Management Team

Although there are exceptions to the rule, it is generally easier to get bigger results faster in smaller companies where implementation is less challenging and there is a lot less politics and far fewer complications.

> "Our Age of Anxiety is, in great part, the result of trying to do today's jobs with yesterday's tools."
>
> – Marshall McLuhan, Canadian literary scholar

I believe it is very important to highlight these challenges in order to understand them, anticipate them and address them.

CHALLENGE: THE "TRAINING DEPARTMENT CAN DO IT" MINDSET

The mother of all obstacles in selecting the right sales management team is when upper management seems to think that the answer to creating a sales culture is mainly resolved by trainers and the training department. This mindset is without doubt the biggest culprit in producing sales failures over and over again.

We have an immense respect for training departments and trainers, many of whom are very capable, dedicated, and caring individuals (in fact, some of our own consultants come from that background). However, they alone can never significantly impact an entire company culture. Following are some of the reasons why.

THE NATURE OF TRAINING

The blunt truth is that a high percentage of operational trainers—many of whom are excellent at what they do—actually know very little about sales, and sales training.

In many instances the trainers that are being used to teach sales were not hired to focus on sales and were not specifically responsible for sales production.

This quickly becomes evident in training classes or during hands-on coaching sessions. Lack of experience in this area also surfaces in training materials, incentive plans and measurement reports. Over time, all this eventually shows up and weakens the entire company's internal sales foundation.

In short, the established "best-practice" standards in many Frontline organizations are often far from it. In fact, in some cases, the use of these poor materials, tools and models actually inhibits the sales effort instead of enhancing it.

Do you know how much money is spent every year on sales training? Over $8 billion! If companies have to recurrently spend this amount every year, how much of that money is being wasted? If you are there scratching your head and wondering why the last $50,000 you spent training your team did not produce results that "stuck," you are not alone. Rob Reed, Owner of a Missouri-based sales and marketing firm found the following:

- *A study at Columbia University that revealed up to 95% of what is taught in training programs is lost in the transfer from education to execution at the point of sale.*

- *A Xerox study several years ago showed that 87% of the knowledge learned in sales training evaporated within 90 days.*

- *A Sales Performance International study of over 6,000 sales professionals showed that most forgot at least 50% of what they learned in training programs in less than five weeks. Over 44% said they forgot it in less than one month. The worst number is that on average, attendees remembered only 16% of the content from sales training workshops after only 90 days.*

Only the full implementation of the KPE will get your training to "stick"! Training, trainers, and the training department play an important but only limited role in making that happen. A fundamental reason for that is the traditional nature of the training role as described below:

> When a trainer delivers an eight-hour classroom workshop, he or she has fulfilled their basic "employment obligation" for the day and earned his or her "keep." In sales performance management, there should be one and only one measure of successful training: quantifiable bottom-line results.

CHALLENGE: THE "THIS IS EASY STUFF" PERCEPTION

The high degree of performance improvement failures in this area is because in many companies the highest levels of management do not perceive Frontline sales as a professional skill. Many corporate leaders feel that selling behind most counters, in contact centers and in retail stores, does not require a complex presentation. Therefore, in their minds, this "rudimentary" customer transaction should be easily facilitated.

The critical disconnect that exists here is in the difference between *the simplicity of the sales transaction itself* and the inherent difficulty of getting an entire Frontline organization to use the process consistently and with outstanding customer care.

CHALLENGE: THE "WE KNOW IT ALL" SYNDROME

Changing or enhancing a culture is a huge undertaking. It requires the participation of many in an organization and the help of outside professionals in many cases with the sales management team at the forefront.

As the training department is charged from above with the responsibility to accomplish the sales training mission, it is naturally resistant to accepting help from other departments or from outside resources. Worse yet, even when there is a realization by upper management that outside help is needed, it is frequently left to the training department to make the decision to assess it and procure it.

In situations where that department head is confident and secure, they are able to make good decisions on the right help to utilize. In many cases, however, insecurity and territorialism sets in and the response of "we can do it ourselves" and/or "they do the same thing we do" prevents forward thinking and growth. Management buys into this confident facade, often to find out two years later (at immense cost to the company) that the actual results were *marginal* at best.

The CFO uses outside accountants, the legal department uses outside law firms, the maintenance crew will call for help when a heating unit is down. It is absolutely okay to use outside help when you need it. The key is to not rely on it exclusively.

CHALLENGE: THE "WRONG BOSS" ISSUE

Surprisingly, an organization will decide to focus on sales, even hiring sales managers or trainers to do so, but then have them report to an operations person. These are often the general managers or regional managers who often know very little about Frontline selling. They may very well be great operators, great marketers, and perhaps even great individual salespeople, but all this requires a far different skill set from the one needed to create a high performance culture at the Frontline.

There are definitely many exceptions to the rule, but in many cases (and we see it repeatedly) it is often the blind leading the blind. So what happens now when the general manager has to provide guidance and development for the trainer? Or worse, what happens when the GM now has to motivate the trainer, train the trainer and the sales manager, give them direction on a daily basis and then hold them accountable? The answer in most cases is "not a whole lot."

Further irony exists when you have trainers reporting to a GM who themselves need to be held accountable for the KPE blueprint implementation. How then do trainers, whose entire financial livelihood is often controlled by the person they report to, rock the boat and hold their boss accountable for implementation?

Frontline sales focus is often uncharted waters for many companies and departments. This entire initiative can be a roulette spin if it is not led by the right people with the right expertise, tools, models and resources. If a manager in charge understands sales and can motivate and develop their trainers, then they as a sales leader can be effective. Unfortunately, in many cases, the new sales managers need training and development themselves. As a result, this common structure proves, in most cases, to be terribly ineffective.

Challenge: The Frontline Managers Can Do It Issue

In most Frontline situations many of the managerial tasks are concentrated solely on meeting the operational needs of the business. Many of the managers have been promoted on that premise and may very well be good operators. Although I do believe that an effective sales manager absolutely needs to "walk the talk" and be able to demonstrate sales successfully on the floor, it is unrealistic to expect this from *all* Frontline managers.

The Frontline manager's role is very important as the manager influences multiple people and is responsible for the daily support of the program. He or she also plays a critical role in setting the tone of expectation for the rest of the team.

An effective way of getting the Frontline managers involved is to give them *specific sales support responsibilities* and then hold them accountable for executing them. These tasks exist in the following areas:

- **Operational Support:** The sales picture quickly becomes clouded if the operation has issues. The Frontline manager's role is to support the salespeople by creating a smooth-running operation that helps facilitate a positive environment for sales. How do you expect a Frontline hotel salesperson to upgrade the customer to a suite if they have no idea whether this inventory is available? It is equally as challenging for a call-center salesperson to sell a bigger and better product if the customer had to hold for ten minutes and then jump through a bunch of hoops to get to a live salesperson.

- **Leadership:** This primarily relates to creating a positive environment. Implementing the elements of The Right Environment, such as lending support, promoting trust, soliciting input, promoting opportunities, and training and development, all have a major impact on sales results.

- **Coaching:** While it is impractical to expect all of your good Frontline managers to be "sales superstars," you should expect them to understand the sales process and demonstrate it when they themselves are on the sales floor. You should also expect that they have a very clear and thorough grasp of the sales process so they can identify weaknesses and solutions to address through effective coaching.

- **Recognition:** The power of a pat on the back is explosive, and it does not require any unique skill or a huge amount of time. Frontline managers who provide frequent and sincere recognition will motivate and inspire their team to continue to reach higher goals.

- **Accountability:** This is perhaps the biggest role that Frontline managers need to play. Ensuring that the Frontline salespeople are held accountable for producing consistently is a responsibility the managers need to enforce on a daily basis.

Transforming Culture Through Three Critical Positions

The Resident Performance Manager, the Champion and the Sponsor are the three absolutely critical positions in this performance formula. Yes, you need all the other managers to step up, but these three positions have the ultimate power to transform the culture at your Frontline. The following section discusses who they are and some of what they need to do.

Avis and Budget's Committed Execution

Larry De Shon EVP of operations fully understood and appreciated the value of every increased cent on his dollar average. With roughly 50 million "opportunity" rental days, an improvement of just $1 per day translated into $35 million in profit contribution annually—and that is after absorbing all costs.

So how does a conglomerate like Avis Car Rental and Budget Rent a Car mobilize and get its 1,000-plus team members at the Frontline to improve their performance and do so in a relatively short period of time? The answer—a committed and dedicated team!

It takes a lot to transform and install a high-performance service based sales culture at the Frontline. It all starts however with the right leadership.

This is the team that sponsored, led and owned their sales culture transformation:

The Sponsor: Larry whose message was clear, direct and very motivational; the revenue potential was a "must have" and the execution of a well outlined program would be rewarded. Equally important was the mandate that "buy in" and support by the field was to be an absolute priority.

The Champion: Gina Bruzzichesi, VP of Human Resources believed in the program and believed in its positive impact on customers and employees. Her dedicated day-to-day involvement in setting up and supporting the infrastructure of a program that would involve 60-plus sales managers became a critical part of the program's success.

The Sales Managers: As "best-practice" standards were defined and customized for all aspects of the program, the main role of the field-support managers was to step up and execute. Many certainly did and the numbers shot up in their cities and regions. Others were slower to come around and a minority just could not cut it.

Sales vaulted 26% resulting in $10M-plus in revenue improvement within 6 months—the fasted large-scale execution and improvement we have seen in our 15 years. Equally as important was the enhanced customer experience and improved employee opportunities. Committed execution— a true win-win for everyone.

Position 1: The Resident Performance Manager (RPM)

In his terrific book, *The E-Myth,* Michael Gerber talks about having an organizational chart with various heads of marketing, sales, accounting, operations, even when you are a one-man show.

When you are small, you play all these roles yourself. You are, however, organized for progressive growth immediately. You have a system and a process in place, which in turn helps you grow. Over time it allows you to bring the right people into your organizations who eventually fulfill these roles.

I would venture to say that regardless of your size, or whether you can afford a Resident Performance Manager, you need to plan for one. In order to forecast the revenue upside and the ROI of this position, apply the formula for sales potential we have used throughout this book.

Adding the tag of "resident" to the performance sales manager may seem a little peculiar to some. The word "resident" means to "serve in a regular full time capacity." I feel there is a certain distinction as well as an element of focus and dedicated responsibility attached to it. I like it, and this is the name we currently use when we place our own Resident Performance Managers on an outsourced basis in companies to help them implement the KPE and quickly achieve maximum sales results.

It would obviously be very nice, and a great bonus, if your Frontline managers were also sales superstars and motivational gurus. If they are, you should consider promoting some of them to the RPM position. However, the reality is that most companies do not have that luxury, and you need to actively search for the right person to fulfill that role.

Choosing the Right Resident Performance Manager

Perhaps it is best to start with who not to choose, because this is perhaps the biggest mistake companies make. Unless they have the qualities outlined below, the Resident Performance Manager should *not* be the trainer, the good operations manager, or someone in the human resources department.

The Resident Performance Manager needs to possess the following qualities:

1. The *SEE factor...* Sincerity, Empathy and a "strong" Ego
2. Strong sales experience
3. Leadership skills
4. The ability to personally connect, motivate, and inspire

5. The ability to demonstrate sales and "walk the talk"

6. A strong understanding of the KPE

7. Passion, intensity, competitiveness, and drive

8. A tenacious focus on results

9. A strong balance between humility and confidence

10. A strong work ethic

11. An ability to handle confrontation and controversy

12. An open mind and a strong desire to learn and grow

As you can see, this is not an easy position to fill. Yes, people who have most of these attributes do exist in the marketplace as well as within organizations. It is virtually impossible, however, to find the individual who possesses all these qualities in their entirety. Once you have identified the right person with most of these qualities, you then must spend the time and resources to train, manage, and motivate that individual.

SHAPING THE RIGHT SALES MANAGER

Here is how to quickly get the best out of your new Resident Performance Manager:

- **Train.** You need to train them on the KPE. You also need to certify them on the right sales seminars and workshops that develop both the Frontline managers and Frontline salespeople. This training should continue on an ongoing basis.

- **Manage.** Regardless of the strength and ability of your Resident Performance Managers, they will not produce to their potential if you are not managing them effectively. It is very easy for people in this position to start splintering their focus with excessive operational tasks; they start running mundane sales reports and fall into "analysis paralysis" instead of doing the hard work on the Frontline. They are, like most of your other employees, in need of daily direction and support.

- **Motivate.** The same KPE elements of motivation apply to getting the most out of your Resident Performance Manager. You need to motivate this person using these three tools:

  » *Recognition:* Celebrate their successes and let them know you appreciate their efforts and contributions to the success of the organization. Keep them excited and engaged by letting them understand the critical role they play and the opportunities they have.

» *An Effective Incentive Plan:* Forget about the pathetic bonus plan most companies have in place. Pay these people great commissions on the sales they help generate. You want a sales manager that is looking for a small salary and a big upside based on producing outstanding results. Help them set and achieve big goals to earn big rewards!

» *Accountability:* The bottom line is *the bottom line.* They need to produce and you need to hold them accountable for doing so. They may look good, talk a good game and light up the room when they deliver a seminar, but if they are not producing results then it does not matter. A capable manager/champion needs to hold the Resident Performance Manager accountable to realistic goals and fully expect that they be met.

Position 2: The Champion

This is the role of the senior person in charge of implementation, the one who trains, manages and motivates the Resident Performance Manager. The Champion can be the owner of the business. In larger companies this role may be assumed by a Regional Sales Manager, who may have up to six RPMs he or she is in charge of leading.

The following critical qualities will help the Champion ensure the success of the Resident Performance Manager, as well as the optimal implementation of the KPE:

- A thorough understanding of the KPE
- A passion for this initiative
- A practical approach to overcoming obstacles
- A genuine appreciation for the Frontline
- A positive relationship with the employees
- Strong leadership
- Strong management skills
- Strong organizational skills
- The ability to motivate
- The willingness to hold people accountable

Position 3: The Sponsor

The Sponsor is the most senior position to whom the Champion reports. The Sponsor oversees the program and ensures its implementation. Although this initiative is only a small part of what he or she does, this leader sets the tone, the priorities, and the pace of the culture change that is desired. The Sponsor could be the president, COO, or CEO of the organization.

Regardless of the size of the organization, the Sponsor has to be the final decision maker. The Sponsor has to be the one who leads this process and ensures the implementation and installation of the KPE. The Sponsor assigns the Right Champions and the Right Plan to ensure the Right Action. The Sponsor also designs the Right Incentive, the Right Recognition Plan and he or she holds the Champions accountable for results.

No matter how badly an organization desires dynamic sales improvement, unless its leader shares the same urgent commitment to the initiative, it is destined to languish and fail. The crushing pressures of change (from technology, competition and globalization) will eventually divert organizational focus and drain the lifeblood of energy from the project.

According to a survey of 1,400 executives and managers conducted by the American Management Association in 2006, 82% of them reported that the pace of change experienced by their organizations has increased compared with five years ago. Further, seven out of ten noted that their organizations experienced disruptive change during the previous year.

So how does a company maintain an acute focus on sales improvement while facing an ongoing barrage of different initiatives? The only way they can do so is to be given the *freedom* to prioritize the sales focus above other organizational "emergencies." And the *power* to do that rests with that one person—the Sponsor.

Who Assumes These Roles in a Small Business?

In a very small business where you have an owner/operator, that owner will have to play all three roles until the business grows. Then, he or she can hire a Resident Performance Manager or a General Manager who can also add the RPM role to his or her area of responsibility.

In a multiple-branch business where the volume in those offices cannot support a Resident Performance Manager, the branch manager must make it a priority to assume that role in the context of his or her other responsibilities. In some cases this person will have to delegate the less profit-impacting tasks to someone else, or eliminate them all together. When you quantify the sales opportunity, I assure you if a significant sales upside does exist—and it usually does—then this exercise will be worth it.

STEP ② Creating the Right Steering Committee

The Steering Committee is the body that drives the creation of a high performance sales culture in the organization. Although the number of participants will obviously depend on the size of the business, the goal is the same: to create ownership and, ultimately, to get the job done. In a typical organization, the steering committee may look like this:

- The Sponsor
- The Champion
- The Resident Performance Manager
- The Training Manager
- Key Operations Personnel

Note: The Steering Committee may request periodic and strategic involvement from people in IT, HR, outside sales and marketing, Frontline salespeople, and others on an "as needed" basis.

It is important not to get too carried away with the number of people on this committee and to only have departments represented that have direct influence on this initiative. This will minimize the number of "chiefs" and eliminate unnecessary delays and confusion. The number of people in the steering committee should never exceed eight.

In smaller organizations, the duties of the preceding positions all still need to be assumed. The only difference is that a single person may have to wear multiple hats for the different initiatives that are identified.

Regardless of the size of the committee, it is often a very good idea to have an objective, outside third party with knowledge in the Khoury Performance Equation to facilitate this process. This will keep it efficient, moving and on task. More importantly, this will provide a valuable sounding board and vetting system for prospective new ideas. This will also provide good resource expertise based on best practices of other industries and a willingness to confront conventional thinking when necessary.

What Does the Steering Committee Do?

The Steering Committee's tasks can be broken down into six areas that I will discuss here and in the next chapter on sales management:

- Contributing to the discovery and gap analysis
- Quantifying the upside revenue potential and setting goals
- Preparation of immediate action plans
- Overseeing the launch and the implementation/execution
- Ensuring accountability
- Ongoing sales management

Unity and ownership are also very critical attributes for a successful steering committee.

Aggressive Ownership

When you bring the various departments that directly influence a single initiative together, a sense of ownership, competition, synergy and pride develops spontaneously. This action and related reaction are critical to the achievement of the goals that have been established. Moreover, positive spillover leads to improved energy, enthusiasm and inter-departmental team building.

Unity

It is vital that all of the key people in the organization understand the importance of creating a sales and service culture, and that they then place this initiative at the very top of their priority list. They then need to perpetually communicate that vision throughout the organization. This vision provides a unifying influence that strengthens as the team wins, loses, struggles and succeeds together.

STEP ③
Performing The Right Discovery

Before you can begin moving toward any destination, you have to know where you stand. This holds true in the realm of building a peak performing sales culture. Evaluating what you are doing now and then comparing your findings to the KPE will emphasize areas of current strength and opportunity. *This is the discovery process.*

Naturally, some discovery has already identified significant sales

> "All truths are easy to understand once they are discovered; the point is to discover them."
>
> — Galileo Galilei

opportunities prior to the sponsor taking on this initiative and forming a steering committee. However, the committee's first task is to identify a discovery team and to discuss the extent and scope of the information they are searching for.

THE DISCOVERERS

In a large organization, the Discovery team can be comprised of the Champion (the day-to-day person in charge of implementation) and one other person. It may also be a good choice to have an outside professional and highly competent third party conduct this discovery. This will allow for less biased reporting and will help employees be more open in their operational and personal feedback.

The Discovery process is achieved primarily through five methods, as shown in Figure 8-5:

- **Observing:** Non-intrusive, simple observation helps ascertain what is going on and how things are managed.

- **Interviewing:** Conversationally "interview" employees in a casual relaxed and non-threatening manner.

- **Focus Groups:** These groups can be made up of a combination of managers and salespeople, or just salespeople. Ensure that these sessions are conducted professionally. Do a lot of listening and very little talking.

- **Fact Finding:** Look closely at policies and procedures on what is expected and how business is generally conducted relative to the 19 critical KPE elements. This also includes analyzing the reporting of data and the trends in revenue, sales, customer service, turnover, production, and so on

- **Employee Surveys:** These are very effective but must be conducted very carefully. I will address this further later in the chapter.

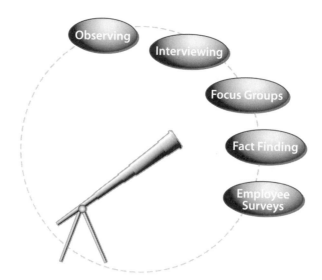

Figure 8-5: The Discovery process is achieved primarily through five methods.

➔ The Gap Analysis

A critical step to achieving a high-performance sales culture will be to apply a gap analysis that compares the current state of your organization to the KPE success formula.

SHORT TERM: THE RIGHT ACTION

Understanding and effectively addressing the gaps in The Right Action elements, usually provides the quickest route to achieving results.

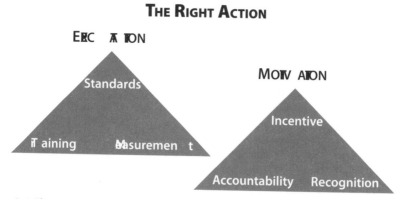

Figure 8-6: The gap analysis takes into account all the variables that play into employee expectation and motivation.

Expectation

Look for the gaps that pose the biggest opportunities. Understanding the current gaps in standards, training and reporting are broken down into the following:

» **Standards**

- Is the current "best-practice" sales process really a best practice?
- Does it employ best practices of other industries that would be perceived as innovative if used in your industry?
- Is it effective?
- How about the sales management process? Is there one?
- Are the training materials sufficient and effective in preparing people to close more sales?
- Are your core training seminars and workshops in place?

» **Measurement**

- Is the organization using the right metric?
- Are sales reports readily available? Are they accurate?
- Are the easy to find and understand?
- Do they rank performance?
- Are they broken down into different products?
- Can everyone run them?
- Can all this be done while measuring service levels that include complaints and compliments?
- Is any performance benchmarking being done either internally between salespeople or externally against other locations?
- What is the spread in sales performance between top performers and average performers?
- What is the spread in sales performance between top performers and bottom performers?

» **Training**

- Who delivers the seminars, the workshops, and the follow-up coaching? Are they delivered well?
- Who manages the sales program? Are they capable and equipped to do so?

- Do your trainers/sales managers have sales credibility? Are you proud and excited to have your sales team made up of a group of your current trainers? If not, why not?
- Is your training practical? Is it solely textbook knowledge or classroom information sharing? How much training do the Frontline salespeople and managers get annually, and how frequently do they receive it?
- What is the amount of time allotted for classroom versus on-the-job training? How is it all conducted?
- Who builds the confidence in your sales team by "walking the talk" on the Frontline?

MOTIVATION

Of course, a successful Frontline has to be highly motivated, and these are the primary factors you need to look for:

» **Incentive (Money)**
  - Is there a commission plan?
  - Is it effective?
  - Does it achieve the right return on investment?
  - Does it reward those who perform accordingly?
  - Is it measurable?
  - Is it simple?
  - Is it understandable?
  - Do the employees know where they stand during or immediately after their shift?
  - Does it penalize low performers?
  - Are the incentives paid in a timely manner?
  - Does the staff trust the incentive plan and how is it measured?
  - How do all of these questions apply to sales managers and Frontline managers?

» **Recognition (Ego)**
  - How often and by what methods are people recognized?
  - Whose responsibility is it to drive the daily motivational spark to the Frontline?

- Are sales boards, contests, accolades and perks used to stimulate excitement?
- Are they effective?
- Are they providing a positive return on investment?
- Are employees desensitized to them or do they legitimately motivate?
- How do managers recognize employees?
- What method and setting do they use?
- Are sales meetings conducted with public recognition?

» Accountability (Fear)

- Does it exist?
- Does it penalize low performers?
- What is the policy on dealing with poor sales and service performance?
- How soon is it applied after substandard performance is recognized?
- Is it applied or do managers look the other way because they need "bodies" on the floor?
- Is it fair? Is it too hard? Is it too soft?
- Is it applied equitably?
- Do the employees fully understand it?
- Is it backed up by a solid training and support process?
- Does it work?

MID-TERM: THE RIGHT FIT

It takes both statistical and intuitive insight to determine if the right people are on the bus. Don't always judge a book by its cover: A salesperson may not appear engaging initially, but if that person is using the right sales process, providing great service and producing numbers, then he or she is a keeper.

Learning who is and is not The Right Fit (as shown in Figure 8-7) requires the "discoverer" to evaluate how well a person matches with the long-term vision of the company. The person who was considered valuable yesterday because they possessed a certain battery of skills may not prove to be valuable tomorrow.

A discovery should give you an idea on the quality of your personnel. However, it cannot serve as a final determination on whether you keep someone or not. As I mentioned earlier you cannot evaluate a Frontline salesperson until you implement many of the elements of the KPE.

THE RIGHT FIT

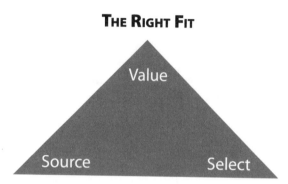

Figure 8-7: It takes both factual and intuitive insight to determine The Right Fit for your business.

Following are the key things to look for when attempting to see how well your company is finding, procuring and retaining exceptional employee talent.

» **Value**

- Is there an understanding, at all organizational levels, of the profit impact and value of a high-performing Frontline employee?

- Is there an appreciation of the ability it takes to generate that sales revenue while still providing fantastic customer care?

- Is this value understood and respected by everyone involved in the selection process?

- Is this understanding translated into a genuine effort to attract and select the "best of the best" for these critical positions?

- Is there an urgency to move people out of the organization whose actions are not consistent with the company's profit and brand-building objectives?

» **Source**

- Do the ads and methods currently being used specifically target salespeople?

- Are they attractive?

- Do they state the upside income potential?

- Has the company identified any reliable sources of strong performers such as the right schools or employee referrals?

- If so, have relationships been built with the right people to leverage those opportunities?

- Determine which of the following categories best fits your recruitment situation and aim for the second:

  » *Passive/informational:* The marketplace is in most cases completely unaware of the opportunities available in your industry and of the financial opportunity it offers to great salespeople in it. Waiting for candidates to knock on your door is a backseat, ineffective approach.

  » *Active/sales-oriented:* Recruitment is based on your managers, sales managers, and human resources people proactively identifying employees in the marketplace via print, the internet or personal experience, and then "selling" them on the benefits of joining your organization.

» **Select**

- Who does the hiring?

- Do the operations and sales managers have any say or involvement in the hiring process?

- Who ultimately has responsibility for how new recruits perform? If the organization has a human resources person, is the HR person making the final decision or are they just performing the initial screening?

- How many and what types of interviews are being conducted? Are applicants clued in to the "good answers" in secondary interviews because they were asked the same questions in previous ones?

- How well is the interview process laid out for the applicant?

- Is the selection process organized, or is the company always making a poor first impression by scrambling around?

- Are the interviewers targeting the key behaviors needed?

Longer Term: The Right Environment

Transforming your current environment into The Right Environment does take time. One of the primary reasons is that an environment has to evolve not only in the field and on the Frontline, but at all levels of management as well. This requires top-down implementation and the participation of *all* senior management, who may not be ready at an early stage to take on this initiative.

One of the most effective ways to learn about the gaps in an environment is to survey employees. This needs to be done at some point, but doing this too early can be precarious: It may raise a dormant issue that you are not prepared to deal with now. A basic principle in employee surveying is not to do it if you are not prepared to address and immediately fix the legitimate concerns employees have at the present time.

The other concern here is that in terms of generating quick results, "The Right Action" part of the KPE provides "low hanging fruit" that can help get things moving quicker and with less initial morale risk. Generally speaking, the higher the current performance, the greater the priority it is to address the environment in order to reach the next level of sales success

A gap analysis of the environment includes evaluation of these critical areas:

- Development
- Communication
- Compensation
- Opportunity
- Support
- Relationships
- Input
- Trust

As I noted previously, an employee survey may be too intrusive at this early stage. More suitable and less complicated methods include passive interviews on the sales floor with the Frontline. Additionally, it is a good idea to gauge senior managers' perspectives and to get their take on the current environment's strengths and weaknesses and the reasons they exist. Other methods for assessing environment gaps, include observation on the sales floor, reviewing policies, procedures reporting and samples of "how things are done." For the qualified observer, this should be sufficient enough information to begin the process.

Once you finish this exercise, you can then take this information and crystallize a picture of where the company is at the present time. This information can then be used to understand what can be done about it, and what plan is needed to transform the team into a Frontline Profit Machine.

STEP ④
• Setting the Right Revenue Goals

Chapter 2 discussed the impact of the Frontline on sales and profits. These are not exaggerated goals or pie-in-the-sky numbers. They are real, they are quantifiable and they are verifiable. For over fifteen years, we have been involved with diverse clients across several continents and in a wide variety of cultures that have realized them firsthand.

Large companies are sometimes shy about disclosing their goals. They seem to fear numbers once they are on paper. That fear may be well-founded. Why? When results are transferred to print, they evolve from a "nice achievement" to a frightening expectation. When there is expectation, lack of achievement now has consequences.

It is not a complicated process to quantify the opportunity. My preference has always been to put the right goal in place and then to dedicate the resources necessary to achieve it rather than implementing a halfhearted, under-resourced job to achieve a weak goal.

Once the goals are agreed on by the committee, it is the job of the Sponsor to keep them at the forefront of the committee member's priorities.

STEP ⑤
• Putting Together The Right Action Plan

It is now time to for the steering committee to reconvene. All the elements of the discovery have to be analyzed with special emphasis on sales performance gaps among the team on the sales floor. The upside potential now has to be quantified and it should serve as the major driver in the efforts moving forward.

Gaps should be addressed through an action plan and broken down in terms of the short-term, mid-term and long-term priorities I discussed earlier.

The program can be launched once the short-term actions are identified, enhanced and/or developed. This then gives you the ability to get it off the ground as quickly as possible. Let's start with the absolute must-haves:

The Right Action Plan:

» **Standards**

- A defined best-practice sales process
- A defined sales management process

» **Measurement**

- Key performance indicators identified and agreed to down to the specifics: average per day, average per ticket, total sales, conversion, incremental sales average, and so on
- A measurement report

» **Training**

- Well-developed and effective sales and sales management seminars
- The right person to deliver these seminars

» **Incentive**

- An effective commission plan
- The plan to introduce it in an upbeat and positive manner

» **Recognition**

- Agreement on the right reasons for recognition
- Agreement on what recognition consists of

» **Accountability**

- Agreement on the need for accountability
- Agreement on the minimum standards of performance
- Agreement on the framework of the critical care program described in Chapter 9. Our usual recommendation is to introduce this 90 days after the initial training and coaching.

STEP ⑥
• Conducting the Right Launch

You have now conducted a thorough discovery. You have a very effective short term plan that addresses The Right Action elements of the KPE. Senior Management is now drooling over the profit potential and the bonuses that come with it. Results are right around the corner.

Before you launch, however, you need to address this new sales focus and the change that can cause anxiety in your staff.

Steve Lemmex, a certified Project Management Professional with 19 years of experience, cites three overriding fears and frustrations that often hamper major change initiatives. You will notice that all of these concerns are anchored in the perceived "loss" or "gain" of power associated with the change.

- *Fear of job loss*
- *Fear of increased responsibility*
- *Frustration with process, whether changes were made without staff input, or with input that was disregarded*

Only when your staff understands how change will affect them personally will these three anxieties dissipate.

GETTING YOUR MANAGERS ON BOARD

Before conducting the first seminars, it is important to put together a one-hour meeting to address the following with your managers:

- **The new direction the organization is taking**
- **The revenue and profit upside potential**
- **Their help in all the logistics for the initial seminars**
- **The benefits and the rewards for them in it**
- **Questions they may have**
- **General feedback from them**
- **Their required energy and enthusiasm about the program**
- **Their help to create the same enthusiasm for the Frontline**

Getting the Frontline Salespeople On Board

This is the critical first step to introducing this new initiative to the salespeople. A two-hour meeting should be set up to discuss:

- The objective of the introduction/enhancement of the new sales focus
- The critical role they play in the future of the company (this should be a strong appeal to their ego)
- An introduction/reintroduction to the key metrics that they will be measured on
- An overview of the key service and sales reports the company will use
- An introduction to the new and enhanced performance-based commission plan with examples of the upside revenue for those who produce
- The scheduling of the launch seminars
- An overview of the training and development that the company is investing in
- An overview of what this initiative will mean in terms of their personal development and future opportunities

Delivering the Initial Core Seminars

The stage has now been set, and now it is time to deliver the two core seminars described below. Frontline salespeople, Frontline managers, the Resident Performance Manager, the Champion and the Sponsor should attend and participate in both seminars. These classes should be scheduled for approximately eight hours each, including lunch and breaks.

An Overview of the Sales Process

The Khoury seminar for this is called *Maximizing Your Impact.*

Description: This seminar is designed to introduce Frontline personnel to The Guiding Principles and the Frontline Service and Sales Process. This interactive course provides a foundation for service-driven profit maximization. Participants will gain a working knowledge of service concepts and key consumer-focused dialogue that will open doors of opportunities for their customers, themselves and the company.

An Overview of the Sales Management Process

The Khoury seminar for this is called *Capitalizing on Sales Management*.

Description: Most every dollar generated by a service and sales operation passes through the hands of its Frontline personnel. The truly successful business is one that provides growth opportunity and supports the Frontline staff in promoting its products and services. This course will provide the management team with tangible tools (e.g., Coaching and Feedback Forms, Daily Game Plans, Rental Logs, Sales Boards, etc.) and techniques necessary to effectively implement the Counter Service and Sales Process. Successful implementation will lead to sustained performance, customer satisfaction, and enhanced profit opportunities.

ENSURING A SUCCESSFUL LAUNCH

Here are some important things to keep in mind to ensure a very successful launch:

- Book a professionally appointed conference room. If you have the appropriate facilities on site, it is critical that you ensure that there are no interruptions whatsoever.
- Provide all the right audio/visual equipment that is needed.
- Make sure that there is quality "higher energy" food and drink
- Ensure that these seminars are delivered in a professional and motivational manner.
- Ensure 100% turnout by planning and scheduling appropriately.
- Ensure that the Sponsor and the Champion introduce both seminars.

STEERING COMMITTEE FEEDBACK

The steering committee should reconvene after the initial launch to discuss the following:

- The formal and informal feedback from the sessions (all class room training should have participant feedback forms)
- Any issues and concerns
- Any updates on the progress of the discovery action plans
- How to keep everyone focused

The steering committee should plan to meet at least once a month or more, if the results are not where they need to be.

STEP ⑦
·•**Ensuring the Right Accountability**

I will repeat myself again by saying that *the biggest challenge that most companies face is to ensure accountability at every level!*

Therefore, the steering committee's biggest job is to ensure the full implementation of the KPE. This starts with the Sponsor who holds the Champion accountable who in turn makes sure the RPM is doing his or her job. All three should then hold everyone involved accountable for implementation and results.

> **ⓘ** Always keep your eyes on bottom-line results! Sales revenue improvement needs to be both the driver and the measure for The Right Action Plan.

➲ We Have Lift-Off.
Now the Journey Begins.

Now you have lift off! If you have done everything correctly, the initial lift from this process, including the launch, should give you an ROI that is at least ten times what you have invested in time and money so far.

This, however, is just the beginning of the journey. Now it is time to measure the results against the short- and long-term goals that have been set. Effective day-in and day-out sales management is an absolute must. That is the subject of the next chapter.

KHOURY KEY TAKEAWAYS

Many companies fail when it comes to the execution phase due to a *lack of preparation, and a lack of understanding and confidence in the potential net profit impact.*

NO-BULL KNOW HOW!
Step 1: Understand the Challenges and Select the Right KPE Sales Management Team
- ✔ The "Training Department Can Do It" Mindset
- ✔ The "This is Easy Stuff" Perception
- ✔ The "We Know It All" Syndrome
- ✔ The "Blind Leading the Blind" Problem
- ✔ The "Frontline Managers Can Do It" Issue

Step 2: Create the Right Steering Committee
- ✔ This is led through the critical role of the three most important positions: the Performance Manager, the Champion and the Sponsor.

Step 3: Perform the Right Discovery and KPE Gap Analysis
- ✔ This important task needs to be done with sensitivity and competence.

Step 4: Set the Right Revenue Goals
- ✔ This critical number should be what sells this initiative and drives it.

Step 5: Put together the Right Action Plan
- ✔ This starts with the elements of the Right Action. Best practice sales processes, accurate reporting, the right training process, an effective commission plan and the right recognition and accountability systems.

Step 6: Conduct the Right Launch
- ✔ Get managers buy-in, get salespeople excited and deliver high-quality launch seminars.

Step 7: Ensure the Right Accountability
- ✔ Without accountability at every level improvement would be marginal at best.

BANKING ON IT!

Most companies have Frontline performance "deficit emergencies." You need to prioritize in terms of the fastest impact. The "low-hanging" fruit exists in the elements of The Right Action. Once this is in place you can then quickly move to finding The Right Fit. Creating The Right Environment is a critical ongoing endeavor to achieving maximum potential.

MANAGING THE MACHINE: FIRING, HIRING, AND INSPIRING

"Great moments are born from great opportunities"

— Herb Brooks

Think big; act small. That's what the greatest companies on earth do. Cultures may be envisioned at a high level, but they are built locally. You can control the creation of your company culture based on what you do with your team and how you affect sales. If you execute this control properly, you will positively affect your team members, your customers, your company and your wallet.

Regardless of the size of your company, in most cases the actual sizes of the individual sales teams are often very manageable. This provides yet another element of control for you on how to positively impact your group.

Still, the sales process can be a beast to manage. That is why you need a plan. In this area, too, the Khoury Performance Equation will serve as a guide to what is missing and what is needed to keep the sales initiative on track. The more of its elements you have in place, the easier it will be to build a consistent and sustainable sales culture.

Just imagine that your team is a piece of art, a sculpture you are creating. You are the artist and you are working on *sculpting* a masterpiece. What you put into this masterpiece is absolutely critical and what you leave out is equally as important.

After marveling at Michelangelo's statue of Goliath-vanquishing David, the Pope reportedly asked the sculptor, *"How do you know what to cut away?" "It's simple"* Michelangelo replied. *"I just remove everything that doesn't look like David."* While I'm not totally sure of its accuracy, this short exchange still offers great insight, that is applicable to sculpting a timeless work of art, or forming a Frontline Profit Machine.

Ultimately, you can boil down the key sales management elements for success to three key strategies shown in Figure 9-1.

THE THREE KEY SALES MANAGEMENT STRATEGIES

FIRING	HIRING	INSPIRING
Biggest weakness provides the biggest opportunity	The shortest route to positive results	Getting your people to perform consistently

Figure 9-1: Three main strategies to drive effective sales management

This final chapter focuses on these key sales management strategies that will allow you to manage the KPE on a daily basis to move forward in your mission, to take your sales through the roof.

🔄 The Big Mistake

What's the biggest impediment to creating a successful sales culture? It is that most organizations believe that if they have sales-process knowledge, then they automatically have the ability to maximize sales results.

This simply is a misconception. If an organization has identified, learned, or copied the right best-practice "sales process," will this somehow translate to getting the team to actually implement this process consistently?

Nope!

If an organization adds training sessions, training manuals, online training programs and trainers, will sales go through the roof?

No again. In fact, that notion is dead wrong. As I mentioned earlier, training is critical, but training alone will not do it.

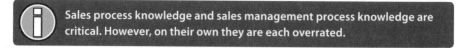

> ℹ️ Sales process knowledge and sales management process knowledge are critical. However, on their own they are each overrated.

The best ideas in the world may be available at the local book store, but just because I study and learn what is in them does not mean I will be able to implement those ideas. Reading Jim Collins' terrific book *Good to Great* ten times and studying what is in it will give you great knowledge, but it will not actually take your company from "good to great."

There are, of course, many layers to implementation beyond acquiring the knowledge of what needs to be done. This includes the following:

 Knowledge can be learned in a classroom, but implementation of that knowledge cannot. That happens in the field and over time.

- Identifying and *sculpting* an outstanding sales management team

- Installing the right Resident Performance Manager, who reports into the right Senior Sales Manager; *the Champion* who has knowledge of the KPE and believes in the process and the outcome

- A Resident Performance Manager, who is certified in the best practice sales training material, also needs to be managed, motivated, recognized, compensated and held accountable for results

Implementation cannot be learned in a training session because sales culture transformation doesn't happen in isolation. It requires flexibility, creativity, good judgment, great people skills, the ability to solve problems, the ability to influence people, and the commitment to deal with challenges.

It also requires passionate leadership, a strong belief in the process and a great understanding of the KPE blueprint. It further requires a steady, consistent approach to achieve great results since mini-initiatives pop up as they always do on a monthly, weekly and even daily basis. Sound like a lot? Very little that is worthwhile is easy.

Aim for What Counts

It is critical that you establish a measurable goal for your effort. An effective discovery should produce a quantifiable revenue number that should fuel your effort to reach upward. At the end of the day, measurement of your progress can be distilled to two critical areas: service and sales, which translate to *results and relationships.*

- **Sales / Results:** The quantifiable bottom-line numbers that you achieve

- **Service / Relationships:** This is first measured by the service you provide your own employees

SALES / RESULTS

Your sales goal, of course, needs to be broken down into monthly and quarterly milestones that would then serve to do the following:

- **Quantify what generally can be categorized as subjective. This includes training and development, hiring, and other seemingly abstract things such as motivation and recognition**
- **Justify the investment in time, money and resources to reach this end goal**
- **Measure the effectiveness of sales management and adjust and react accordingly**
- **Hold all parties accountable for the progress**

SERVICE / RELATIONSHIPS

The service aspect of selling is critical; it is the foundation of the sales process. This foundation begins at home within your organization and for your own team.

This is the "inspirational" part of the sales management process and the heart of it is the positive environment that is created for your team—the group that will make your customers happy and make your P&L statement even happier.

Internal focus on your own employees is measured through:

- **Employee surveys**
- **Turnover**
- **How your employees service your customers**
- **Sales and your bottom line**

Once your goal is set and the launch has been successfully performed, it is time to *sculpt the team into a Frontline Profit Machine.*

⤳ Firing: The Profit Contribution Report and Critical Care

I chose to start with the subject of "firing" for two reasons:

The first is to highlight the critical importance of doing this. As I mentioned earlier, you really don't know the strength of your team until you implement a significant portion of the KPE. Doing that would result in some unexpected positive performance by some you did not think had it in them. However, you will still have weak performers who will always drag your numbers down. This group needs to be addressed immediately if you want the kind of change that leads to peak performance. This is most companies' biggest failure and that's why I chose to begin with it.

The second reason I begin with this is because you cannot fire someone based on performance unless you can measure *how they are performing*. The Profit Contribution Ranking Report (PCR) discussed later provides that ability and also serves as a powerful foundation for effective sales management, including the critical element of accountability.

First, let's look at two examples of employees you *won't* be firing.

JOE, THE SALES GUY

Look at the top Frontline salespeople. Joe is at the top again, month-in month-out. Joe is in the top 10% of performers. He has a great attitude, and sure enough, he came in from another industry possessing far less experience than many of your more tenured team members who have been there for years.

Joe also has other things he has less of: far less bad attitude, and far less negative thinking. In fact he is downright positive; Joe looks forward to being at work and has a great service-focused approach to selling.

Joe has been able to perform at an incredibly high level, whether he works the day shift or the night shift. He also performs well when he works in your downtown branch or out in the suburbs. Not only does he have incredible sales results—his customers love him.

DANIELLE, THE BRANCH MANAGER

Look at the different branches in your territories, or the different departments in your business. Look at the variance in sales performance in these branches and departments. Rank them and measure performance against your respective expectations and budgets.

Look at Danielle's location. Sure enough, it always ranks at the top. Danielle has moved to three different branches in the last two years, and every time she runs a new store she is able to turn it around.

She proves that the excuses the previous managers had were wrong. Danielle consistently shatters the notion the other managers peddle when they claim that the reason their stores are not hitting their goals is because "customers are different here."

Not only do Danielle's stores perform at the top, but her employees respect her and look up to her leadership. She is an incredible positive influence and has been responsible for the promotion of three managers who have worked under her.

THE SILVER LINING

Wow, how fantastic would your businesses and life be if all you had working for you are Joes and Danielles! Wouldn't it be great if they were also easy to find?

Unfortunately, business and life do not work that way. But what you might not know is that there is a huge silver lining to this truth: If Danielle and Joe were easy to find and groom, everyone would do it, and there would not be a competitive edge in finding them and bringing them into your operation.

You will not be able to have all Joes and Danielles, but I promise that you can do a lot better than some of the severely under-performing salespeople you currently employ. Weeding out those employees starts with a very important part of any effective sales management process: the PCR.

➋ The Profit Contribution Report

The Profit Contribution Report (PCR) is an internal management tool that cuts to the heart of the numbers. It clearly lets you know who is contributing to your success and who is not. It then puts the responsibility on the managers to address these issues quickly and effectively.

Initially, this sales management report is not to be shared publicly with the Frontline. Over time, and as you give your team the right support and the tools to succeed, you may then be able to share it with them on an individual basis.

Figure 9-3 shows a sample PCR, with the following graphic delineation for performance categories:

- Top and strong performers: white
- Good performers: light gray
- Performers who require additional coaching and attention: dark gray
- Performers who require *critical care:* white type against dark gray

Retail Store	
Full-time Team Members	**Sales June**
Top 25%	
Joe	$ 50,000
Jill	$ 48,000
Jim	$ 47,000
Jack	$ 43,000
Jane	$ 41,000
Avg.	**$ 45,800**
Sally	$ 38,000
Sara	$ 37,500
Susan	$ 36,000
Sam	$ 33,000
Sandra	$ 32,000
Avg.	**$ 35,300**
Tom	$ 28,000
Terry	$ 26,500
Tim	$ 24,000
Tony	$ 23,000
Tara	$ 22,000
Avg.	**$ 24,700**
Bottom 25%	
Mark	$ 21,000
Matt	$ 19,500
Mandy	$ 15,000
Molly	$ 13,500
Major	$ 11,000
Avg.	**$ 16,000**

Top 25% vs. Bottom 25% – Financial Impact		
Average Sales Gap	Month Total Lost Revenue	Annual Potential Loss
$ 29,800	$149,000	$1,788,000

Bottom 25% vs. Location Average			
Location Average	Sales Gap	Month Total Lost Revenue	Annual Potential Loss
$30,450	$14,450	$72,250	$867,000

Figure 9-3: A Sample Profit Contribution Ranking Report

ANALYZING THE REPORT

- The bottom 25% salespeople produced less than $149,000 in sales in the month of June than the top 25% did, translating into $1,788,000 in annual lost revenue.

- This same group produced $72,250 less than the location average for the month, which amounts to $876,000 in lost revenue annually.

CAN YOU AFFORD TO LOSE THIS REVENUE?

If this is revenue you are prepared to lose, then I sincerely apologize; you have been reading the wrong book. But if you—like most companies—could desperately use this revenue, then start by designing and customizing your own PCR report along the lines of the preceeding example.

If your sales force is too small or too inexperienced, then design this report to compare their performance against an acceptable sales average or another target representing the realistic sales goals you believe they should be aiming for. Make sure these numbers are accurate as the effectiveness of this report greatly diminishes if you have either unrealistic or weak expectations.

The PCR and the KPE

This report now becomes the basis for driving numerous KPE elements as well as many sales management initiatives including:

- **Providing recognition for those at the top**
  - » Understanding who your top performers actually are
  - » Valuing the top performers and their contribution

- **Evaluating the recruitment process**
  - » Profiling top performers
  - » Soliciting referrals from top performers
  - » Evaluating the various sources from which you are recruiting
  - » Evaluating your recruitment needs

- **Understanding the impact of the performers and the effectiveness of the incentive plan**
  - » Are the minimum levels of commission pay tiers in line?
  - » Are you paying the bottom performers too much?
  - » Are they satisfied with what they automatically get?
  - » What is the ROI on your commission plan?
  - » Which salespeople give you the best return and with which do you keep the most revenue after their production and compensation?

- **Evaluating the effectiveness of the training to include:**
  - » The need for more seminars and workshops
  - » The effectiveness of the new hire training
  - » The effectiveness of the Resident Performance Managers
  - » The effectiveness of the Frontline Managers support
  - » The trends in performance on different shifts
  - » The training and coaching plan: who you need to spend time with and who is a waste of time

- **The most important contribution of the PCR is to quantify the effectiveness of Frontline salespeople, Frontline management, and RPM and Champion accountability**
  - » The financial variance number on the teams production does create a higher sense of urgency to get things done at multiple levels.
  - » It illuminates the ability to impact profit through a channel that you totally control.

> » It lets you know who on your team is in need of urgent and immediate *critical care!*

As you can see, the impact of this report is far reaching. It provides the best tool I know of to manage sales on a daily basis as well as to ensure the implementation of the elements of the KPE over time.

ACCOUNTABILITY AND CRITICAL CARE

The numbers have spoken. In fact, the PCR is screaming at you! You have team members who are murdering your bottom line! What are your minimum acceptable standards of performance? If you don't have minimum standards, and many companies don't, then you need to establish them and you need to do so quickly.

I understand that selling may not have been an expectation in the past, and some of your Frontline representatives were not hired to be salespeople, but this is a new day!

You now realize that you cannot afford not to move forward with creating a sales and service culture. You also recognize that achieving better sales performance in an area of the business you actually control is not an option; it is a necessity!

BUT SALLY IS SO NICE

I know that some of the low performers are good friends, good employees, and they have been working for the company for years. I promise you, however, that they are in the lower tier because they are not trying very hard. In many cases, they are not trying at all.

If they are simply unable to sell but are good employees, then perhaps you can find them another job in your company. Otherwise, you should help them find another job working for someone else.

CRITICAL CARE: BECAUSE IT'S AN EMERGENCY

The first remedy for those who don't achieve this minimum level of expectation is recurrent training. I like the name *critical care* because it combines a sense of urgency with a message of support.

Critical care is a series of training classes to get lower performers to improve. It also provides these individuals more attention on the sales floor and in coaching sessions.

You really don't know how strong your salespeople are until you at least implement the short-term "Right Action" elements of the KPE. If you are implementing new minimum sales standards, I would not place people in *critical care* until 90 days after the launch of the program.

You do have to get feedback from human resources and your legal counsel on the specifics of the program and how long of a time period you have to place consistent low performers in *critical care* before you let them go.

ACCOUNTABILITY: IT'S NOT JUST FOR SALESPEOPLE

Accountability is an equal opportunity event. It is not just for the salespeople. The influence of various managers on this program is even more important. Accountability needs to be addressed at multiple levels:

- **Sponsor holds the Champion accountable**
- **Champion to RPM**
- **Champion to Senior Managers**
- **RPM to Frontline Managers**
- **RPM to salespeople**
- **Frontline Managers to salespeople**

Please refer to Chapter 6 for more details on accountability and *critical care*. Once you have given your salespeople and managers all the support and training needed to improve, it is time for them to either move their performance up or to time for you to move them out.

URGENCY: IT'S YOUR CALL

At the end of the day, the most successful companies find a way to address key challenges quickly and efficiently. Larger companies have a much harder time with this since bureaucracy, red tape, and fear of legal issues inevitably creep up.

As I mentioned earlier, it is entirely your decision on how aggressive or soft you want to be in your "move up" or "move out" strategy. But whether you are strong or lenient, your company's sales potential will never be fully realized without an accountability program that replaces low performers.

The greatest organizations are those that usually think big but act small, and therefore are able to *react* more quickly. It is up to you to address the group that is severely hurting your numbers and your profits. The faster you do that, the faster you will sculpt a high-performance team at your Frontline.

Hiring: Three Effective Strategies

Turnover and the *transition performance-gap cost that accompanies it,* along with the cost of low performers as measured by the PCR, are realities that erode your organization's profit tremendously.

THE CASE FOR OVER-HIRING

Establish a good variable incentive plan with a low base and a higher commission payout based on higher production. Then ask yourself whether you can afford *not* to always be looking for superstars. Can you afford to pass up even one when you do find him or her? At the very least, you know you need to keep potential "superstar" new hires engaged and on your radar screen when you come across them.

Only you can put the numbers to it to decide when it is in your best interest to replace a struggling performer with a person who has greater potential. Our experience shows that when you find that superstar, you should bring him or her onboard. If you have the right pay plan, these top producers, while they may make the biggest checks, are in the end your least expensive employees and by far your best value.

FROM PASSIVE TO PROACTIVE RECRUITMENT

You and your managers should be on the lookout for prospective talent in your local market at all times. Understand your Unique Recruitment Proposition and arm yourself with some business cards and *a great two-minute verbal commercial* about why your company is an exceptional employer, and go!

Proactive recruitment means you find your new team members. It means you are on the constant lookout for talent. You will find these people while you are shopping, dining, or working out. You find them while you are running errands, on your way to a business meeting or sitting in your doctor's waiting room.

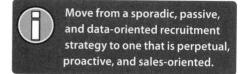

Move from a sporadic, passive, and data-oriented recruitment strategy to one that is perpetual, proactive, and sales-oriented.

Look for potential top sales producers who can function well in a Frontline environment in these areas:

- Valet stands (a popular job for many hard working students)
- Good steak houses and other high-end restaurants
- Clubs or lounges
- "Employee of the Month" walls in many types of businesses
- Travel desks, airline offices, car rental offices and hotels
- Car dealerships
- Retail establishments
- Mall stands

These are just a few suggestions—you never know when or where you might run across a great candidate. You build a top-performing team by always having your recruiting radar up!

Right Compensation = Effective Recruitment

Implementing the KPE helps introduce a higher level of performance that then justifies a higher level of performance-based compensation. Combined, these factors then create a terrific opportunity for the potential sales-oriented (and hopefully money-driven) candidate. The following are a few examples:

Car Rental Agent

This is typically a $12 per hour job. The impact of a top producer in a higher-volume airport can be $100,000 a year in profit. Ten higher-producing agents can completely transform the profit of a location.

A commission-based compensation plan can help easily justify another $15 per hour for top performers. This now becomes a $50,000 a year job, bringing in a whole new level of applicants and drawing professionals from the mortgage industry, the real-estate industry, the car sales industry, etc.

Call-Center Sales Agent

For a higher-ticket item it is not uncommon to have up to a $1,000,000 swing between high performers and low performers in many contact centers. If the ticket item is lower, the profit margin is usually still very substancial.

Look back on the example of the PCR report I introduced earlier. The top 25% of your team is making money for you, while the bottom 25% is killing your profits. Based on this simple fact, you can now easily justify paying those at the top three times their minimum base pay in commission.

This transforms the profile of the salesperson you are seeking. Your expectations for qualifications can now become significantly higher, resulting in much higher sales production and exponentially more profit.

Remember that no one step alone generates maximum sales results. Maximizing profits and reaching potential can happen only through the implementation of the KPE in its entirety.

Mastering the recruitment process to help *sculpt* your Frontline team into a money machine is an investment in the long-term sustainability and growth of your business.

⟳ Inspiring: Making it Happen Day In and Day Out

You've laid the groundwork for creating The Right Environment. You've ensured The Right Fit by inviting potential top performers into your organization. Parts of your Frontline Profit Machine are in place. Now you need some inspiration to make it all happen.

> "The task of leadership is not to put greatness into people, but to elicit it, the greatness is there already."
>
> — John Buchan

Arguably, almost anything you do relating to the KPE can be inspirational, but this inspiration will happen only as long as your actions are done professionally, and with the best interest of your customers, your employees, and the company in mind.

Some actions are more inspirational than others. Let's discuss these actions as they relate to the different elements of the KPE.

THE RIGHT ENVIRONMENT

A *Time* magazine article in April 2008 shared a study by Towers Perrin of 40 multinational companies. The findings were very telling. Companies with high employee engagement scores had the following results:

- Operating margins were 5.75 *percentage points* higher than those of low-engagement companies.
- The same companies had net profit margins that were 3.44 *percentage points* higher.

Now imagine the profit-busting impact of combining that type of engagement with the sales focus and sales management system that we are discussing in this book.

In order to identify the elements of worker engagement, Gallup conducted many thousands of interviews of multiple organizations of all sizes and types across numerous

> A positive environment is not a warm and fuzzy thing that is "nice to have." It is good business and the right thing to do.

industries and countries. The 12 statements shown in Figure 9-4, called the Gallup Q12, emerged from Gallup's pioneering research as those that best predict employee and workgroup performance. Most of these statements can be correlated to KPE elements found in the KPE Right Environment model (Figure 9-5).

#	Gallup Q12 - Worker Engagement and Performance Predictor	Primary KPE Element
1	I know what is expected of me at work.	Communication
2	I have the material and equipment I need to do my work right.	Support
3	At work I have the opportunity to do what I do best every day.	Support
4	In the last seven days I have received recognition or praise for doing good work.	Recognition
5	My supervisor or someone at work seems to care about me as a person.	Trust
6	There is someone at work who encourages my development.	Development
7	At work my opinions seem to count.	Input
8	The mission or purpose of my company makes me feel my job is important.	Trust
9	I have a best friend at work.	Relationships
10	My fellow employees are committed to doing quality work.	Trust
11	In the last 6 months someone at work has talked to me about my progress.	Development
12	This last year, I have had opportunities at work to learn and grow.	Opportunities

Figure 9-4: The Gallup G12 survey identified the top levels of worker engagement.

Figure 9-5: The Right Environment as defined in the Khoury Performance Equation

The only thing that is missing in the Q12 is the element of compensation. However, in dedicated sales positions—those that we are addressing in this book—it is a key element in The Right Environment. If it is not, you have the wrong person on your sales team who at best is very inconsistent in his or her sales performance and more than likely is dragging your numbers down.

APPLY THE RIGHT ACTION ELEMENTS TO GET THE RIGHT ENVIRONMENT

Let's walk the talk and apply the KPE to achieve our intended objective. In this section we will focus on creating The Right Environment for your salespeople through the primary group responsible for doing so, your Frontline managers.

Apply the elements of The Right Action to get the managers to create The Right Environment.

Expectation: Standards for The Right Environment

What are your standards when it comes to creating The Right Environment?

- Development
- Compensation
- Communication
- Opportunities

- Support
- Relationships
- Input
- Trust

Understand the gaps that exist. Create an action plan around them. Address them, revive them or enhance them. You will be surprised at the impact of even baby steps in this area.

Expectation: Training for The Right Environment

It is critical that your Frontline Managers understand that their primary role is not that of daily task master. Anyone can do that; their specialized role is that of a revenue-generating leader.

Train your managers to be the leaders they have the potential to be. Here is a sample of some of the seminars and workshops that we deliver for our clients in this area:

- Capitalizing on Sales Management
- Coaching through Leadership (basic and advanced)
- Analyzing the Numbers
- Finding The Right Fit
- Elements of Effective Communication (working with all varied personality types)
- Winning by Working Together (team bonding)
- Macro Management (eliciting peak performance by tying employee personal goals to company goals)

Expectation: Measurement for The Right Environment

Create simple surveys that reflect the KPE Right Environment elements. Encourage your employees to fill these out. Create a confidential environment where your associates can be brutally honest.

Spend more time on the sales floor with the team as well as one-on-one time with your salespeople. Conduct focus groups on a quarterly basis initially, and then you can move to a biannual and annual basis. Keep track of all the feedback you get. You will quickly find a direct correlation between better feedback and higher sales.

Motivation: Incentive for The Right Environment

Include the survey results as part of the managers' compensation plan.

> **i** Reward Frontline leaders who create happy employees, who then work hard to make your external customers happy, satisfied and loyal.

Obviously this has to be only one component of their entire bonus and commission package.

Motivation: Recognition for The Right Environment

Recognize the managers who are your true leaders on the sales floor and in the field. Your most valuable asset is those managers who develop, train, coach and motivate their people to achieve sales targets and company goals. Appreciate them, thank them, and recognize them!

Motivation: Accountability for The Right Environment

You may have a manager who is lethargic; employees don't like him; he is nowhere to be found, and he has the people skills of doormat. He may have it in him to do better, but unless he is held accountable for facilitating a better environment, you have no chance of reforming him! Enough said.

YOU NEED THE RIGHT ENVIRONMENT FOR EVERYONE

The Right Environment is a function of the culture that exists in the entire company. You cannot have a bad environment for your managers and expect them to be outstanding leaders on the sales floor.

Apply the same process for the senior managers who lead the Frontline managers. This will quickly become an inherent attribute of your organization, part of your company culture, and part of "how you do things" every day.

THE RIGHT TRAINING AND COACHING

I described the initial introduction to the sales process and the sales management "launch" seminars in Chapter 8. Once that is complete, it is imperative to quickly spend one-on-one time with the Frontline people on the sales floor.

The initial seminars are part training, and a bigger part is getting the Frontline to believe in the value of their products, their services and their new role as sales professionals.

For many on the Frontline, high-level selling is new, and it can be scary. Their confidence may be fragile, so seeing a competent Resident Performance Manager demonstrating the sales process immediately after the classroom training is a very important step that will make a huge difference.

Train, coach, motivate, embrace, encourage and reinforce the positive aspect of service-based selling on the sales floor immediately and throughout the training process!

PRESENCE

Presence is just that: being present where it all happens. Where your customers are: the ones who are on your payroll and the ones who buy and use your services.

Here's a problem: For all too many senior managers, middle managers, Frontline managers and astoundingly, even trainers and sales managers, the Frontline is just not where they want be and therefore not where they are usually found.

Senior managers are "too busy" with more important "high-level strategy." Middle managers have critical HQ requests and a schedule full of meetings and conference calls. Frontline managers have to keep the operation going with a litany of tasks, *all* of which have to be done in the "back office." The trainers and sales managers have to "run reports" to see where "the numbers" are, but the good news is they really do mean to spend more time on the sales floor and plan to definitely "get to it" very soon.

While I understand that different management roles do have other responsibilities, *every* manager needs to spend some time where it all happens: at the Frontline.

THE CHIEFS ARE NOWHERE TO BE FOUND

The worst culprits of this lack of presence are often the trainers and sales managers themselves. Part of the reason we call that position "Resident" Performance Manager is because they have to be "resident" on the sales floor. Additionally one of the reasons we place Resident Performance Managers in client companies is because we observed their sales numbers spike 10%, 20% and 30% on average on the days that our consultants were *present* on their sales floor. That is where your sales manager has to be resident! After classroom training and recruiting, that time on the floor should amount to 80% of his or her work schedule.

Why, specifically, should *all* managers spend time on the sales floor? To provide feedback, motivation, recognition, observation, trust, development, and support, just to name a few benefits. I could go on to name many more—being around customers and employees helps every element of the KPE.

Daily Game Plans

The daily game plan, shown in Figure 9-6, is a critical sales management tool that lets everyone know exactly what they're expected to do.

DAILY GAME PLAN – Jacks Sports Town Sat. July 12 2008			Notes/Comments
Month To Date Stats			
Goals	Actual	Variance	
Revenue $600,000	$675,000	($75,000)	
Ticket Average $48.00	$51.00	$3.00	
Conversion 30%	32%	2%	
Yesterday Stats			
Goals	Actual	Variance	
$50,000	$53,000	$3,000	
$55.00	$52.00	($3.00)	
32%	33%	1%	
Store Comments			
Great day! Thank you!			
Let's shoot for $58.00 today!			
Top down sell!!!			

Yesterdays Stars	Top Revenue	Comments
Joe	$2,500	Wow! Record for the month
John	$1,700	Terrific work John
	Top Ticket Average	Comments
Danielle	$71.36	Way to top down sell... Incredible number!
Joe	$65.70	High Ticket = High Revenue = Big $$Paycheck
Today's Plan		
CUSTOMIZE to include operational issues ... specials ... sales tips ... inspirational quotes		
Important Notes		
CUSTOMIZE to include key selling points, ... stats ... urgency matters ... customer service notes/stats ... store recognition		
Month To Date Stars	Top Revenue	Comments
Joe	$30,000	Record pace!
John	$28,000	Outstanding!
	Top Ticket Average	Comments
Danielle	$68.98	Fantastic work!
Joe	$65.70	Terrific job!
Team Corner		
CUSTOMIZE to include, birthdays, employment anniversaries, special recognition, special employee family and business announcements, social events, on going contests and so on		

Figure 9-6: The Daily Game Plan is an essential tool for keeping your Frontline on track.

You will need to customize your daily game plan to the type of business you have and the nature of what you are selling. Whether you are able to do an electronic version or you have to write a daily game plan by hand, many of the core messages mentioned above have to be communicated.

As you can see from the abbreviated sample, it also serves to positively reinforce so many of the elements of the KPE. This includes communication, recognition, support, training, measurement and others, depending on what you need to emphasize and enforce.

THE RIGHT INCENTIVE

Frontline sales usually involve a high number of transactions. A contact center salesperson can take over 100 calls a day, while a retail salesperson may interact with over 150 people a day; a lot of "no thanks" are imbedded in those transactions.

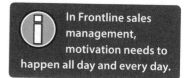

In Frontline sales management, motivation needs to happen all day and every day.

   It is therefore critical that the incentive plan generates a lot of enthusiasm and motivation. However, it does have to make sense for both the team member and the company.

Incentive Considerations

I've discussed the importance of an effective commission plan. It is critical from a sales management perspective that you have answers to the following key ten questions:

1. Does the commission plan use the critical metrics I need to make money as a company?

2. Does it pay my top producers very well on a performance based plan?

3. Are my top producers my best value; do I keep significantly more after I pay them the biggest checks?

4. Is this a simple plan to understand? If I was to test the Frontline, would at least 90% of those that have been around for more than six months understand the plan? (This is a great barometer of the level of sales focus you have; our experience shows that 80% of companies would not pass this test.)

5. Does it allow the Frontline to know what their commission is trending on a daily basis?

6. Does the commission plan account for service levels and encourage a positive service-based sales approach?

7. Does the plan help recruit and retain top talent?

8. Does the plan perpetuate the goal of creating The Right Environment?

9. Do all levels of management understand the plan and do they support it?

10. Do many of these same questions apply in reference to the commission plan for Frontline managers and the Resident Performance Manager?

The CEO Who Wears a Name Tag

How does a company that grosses $55 billion annually, and operates over 460 stores in 37 states and eight countries, not spend a penny on PR, marketing, or advertising? The answer, according to Jim Sinegal, CEO and founder of Costco, is because his loyal work force does the promoting for them.

As he explained to ABC News, *"We have 120,000 loyal ambassadors out there who are constantly saying good things about Costco."*

The story of Costco's success has many chapters, but the one to start with is Sinegal's leadership.

Here are just a few things that depict his activities and characteristics:

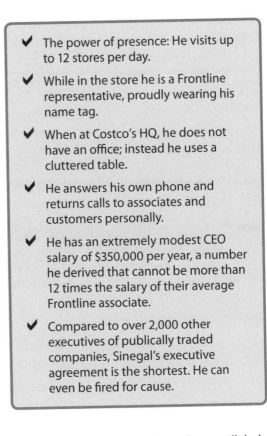

- ✔ The power of presence: He visits up to 12 stores per day.

- ✔ While in the store he is a Frontline representative, proudly wearing his name tag.

- ✔ When at Costco's HQ, he does not have an office; instead he uses a cluttered table.

- ✔ He answers his own phone and returns calls to associates and customers personally.

- ✔ He has an extremely modest CEO salary of $350,000 per year, a number he derived that cannot be more than 12 times the salary of their average Frontline associate.

- ✔ Compared to over 2,000 other executives of publically traded companies, Sinegal's executive agreement is the shortest. He can even be fired for cause.

Does creating The Right Environment work? Perhaps these facts will help answer that question. Costco has become the nation's fourth-largest retailer with 45 million visitors each year. They promote almost entirely from within, which results in turnover that is arguably the best in retailing. And they are one of the few success stories of the hard-hit retail sector in 2008.

Monitor these questions and react accordingly to any gaps that exist. In a sales environment, you want the incentive plan to be a big deal. It needs to drive your Frontline and it needs to do so … you guessed it … day in and day out!

Performance-Based Scheduling

In Frontline selling, operations are often open 12 hours a day. Some are 24 hours a day, and most are open on weekends and many holidays. You better believe that a team member's schedule is a big issue. How that schedule is set can have a huge impact on both the employee and the company.

From an employee's standpoint, the top performers may love the idea of a schedule that offers more sales opportunities. The majority, however, may want the most convenient "lifestyle" schedule they can get.

That lifestyle could be for a student that needs to fit in his or her school schedule, a mom or dad who may be concerned with child care, or a single person who wants to go clubbing on Saturday night. In many instances these needs are real and in some cases, especially for part timers, you have no choice but to appease their scheduling requirements.

Having said all that, you need to work through these concerns and as much as possible implement the type of schedule that allows you to place *Top Performers at Top Locations at Top Times.*

> The facts are overwhelming: Implementing a performance-based scheduling strategy, or some form of it, will result in an incredible boost to your bottom line.

Structuring Your Sales Lineup

Great leaders put their players in positions to win. If you were managing a major league baseball team, and you were setting your hitting lineup for the day, where in the batting order would you place your best "on-base" hitter and run-scorer? Where would you place your best home-run hitter?

Obviously, you would place your best "on-base" person at the top of your lineup. Why? You would want to give him the most "opportunities" to do exactly what he does best: get on base and score runs. Additionally, you would bat your home run-hitter in the "cleanup spot," fourth, so he can "clean up the bases" with what he does best, hit home-runs and drive runs in.

Now, imagine batting these two exceptional players 8th and 9th at the bottom of your lineup, where they would get the least amount of opportunity. "Well, that's not smart; why would anyone do that?" you may ask. You would just be setting up your team for failure. Exactly, but sales managers do it every day!

In short, you need to strive for a "3T" strategy: *Top Performers at Top Locations at Top Times.* Figure 9-7 shows an example of the potential impact "3T" scheduling can have.

Retail	Clothing	
Store Hours	Monday – Saturday Sunday	8 am to 9 pm 10 am to 6 pm
	Type of Shift	*Traffic Count*
	AM / mostly week-day shift PM / mostly weekend shift	30% 70%

Seniority or Shift bid Scheduling				
Top Performer on AM Shift				
Joe	*Conversion* 25%	*Average Ticket* $95		
	AM shift customer count	Sales revenue/shift	Per month	Per year
Joe's Results	60 Customers sold 15	$1,425	$28,500	**$342,000**

Low Performer on PM Shift				
Sam	*Conversion* 14%	*Average Ticket* $75		
	PM shift customer count	Sales revenue/shift	Per month	Per year
Sam's Results	140 Customers sold 19.6	$1,470	$29,400	**$352,800**
			Total Sales	**$694,800**

Performance-Based Scheduling				
Flip Schedules				
Low Performer on Am Shift				
Sam	Conversion 14%	Average Ticket $75		
	AM shift customer count	Sales revenue/shift	Per month	Per year
Sam's Results	60 Customers sold 8.4	$630	$12,600	$151,200

Top Performer on PM Shift				
Joe	Conversion 25%	Average Ticket $95		
	PM shift customer count	Sales revenue/shift	Per month	Per year
Joe's Results	140 Customers sold 35	$3,325	$66,500	$798,000
			Total Sales	$949,200

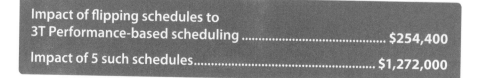

Impact of flipping schedules to
3T Performance-based scheduling $254,400
Impact of 5 such schedules.. $1,272,000

Figure 9-7: 3T Scheduling is an important tool that you can use to assure that you get the most out of your top performers.

The application in contact centers for those rare companies that know it and are able to pull it off is called "skilled-based routing." This is where the top "revenue opportunity" calls are sent to the top performers resulting in exponentially positive sales results.

THE KPE TIE-IN, AGAIN

3T scheduling may not be possible in some companies. In others, a gradual move is entirely possible, but there may be union issues that may prevent this. There may be precedent that complicates it as well as an array of other challenges that may exist. That's why, at the risk of sounding like a broken record, I continue to repeat the importance of the interdependency of the KPE blueprint. If the communication is there, the trust is evident, the support levels are high, the commission plan is generous for producers, and the opportunities for growth are abundant, an eventual move to 3T scheduling becomes a lot easier.

Monitor the schedule, understand the impact and ensure that the KPE elements are in place. Move then to support the right changes to enable a 3T scheduling approach.

Help motivate and inspire your team to move their numbers. This eases the transition to 3T scheduling and consequently facilitates a move in the right direct for company profits.

RECOGNITION

As I have mentioned throughout this book, hire people with the *SEE factor* (Sincere, Empathetic, and with a "strong" Ego).

A strong ego usually comes with a person who is driven, competitive, wants to be at the top, and has an unwavering persistence to be successful. That kind of ego has to be stroked and fed on an ongoing basis—when the person deserves it.

As a sales manager, it is important that you ask yourself some of the following questions and react accordingly:

- **Do sales scoreboards exist and are they updated daily?**
- **Does the daily game plan have the right recognition elements from the previous day and throughout the month?**
- **Do you have monthly plaques for the top service-based salesperson? (Top sales is defined as having high-revenue performance with zero to minimal customers service complaints depending on the nature of your business)**
- **Are your managers catching people "doing something right" on the sales floor?**
- **Are they, when justified, recognizing everyone to help encourage and move average and low producers to higher levels?**
- **Are they recognizing all producers for meeting their monthly goals?**

Feeding the ego is an essential element of successful sales management. This needs to be done by all levels in management, for *all team members* that deserve it and at every level of the organization.

Ensure that this is done day-in and day-out to keep that strong, ego-driven machine well-oiled and producing great numbers!

> "I want to be what I've always wanted to be: dominant."
>
> — Tiger Woods

GOAL SETTING

In many companies, goal setting has been reduced to a task that has to get completed by a certain date and is delegated to a manager or supervisor who has a hundred other competing tasks to finish. In many cases the manager completes the goals using generic corporate targets and hands it to the salesperson. In some cases goals are completed two to three weeks into the month for that month. Some go as far as having the salespeople fill out their own goals and then throw that sheet into the "goal file" with no discussion about their targets. If goal setting is nothing but a mundane task, throw it out.

Written monthly goal setting is a critical part of performance management and bottom-line results.

Effective goal settings should have the following items in place:

- An open discussion between your Frontline sales force and your sales manager
- An uninterrupted time slot where the RPM reviews the previous month's performance as well the performance vs. their peer group
- A candid discussion about the three key motivational drivers: ego, money and accountability
- A review of performance
- A discussion on how daily efforts lead to the monthly target
- A discussion on earning opportunities: how their monthly incentives add up to annual earnings
- A motivational opportunity to discuss what reaching these revenue goals through baby steps can mean in terms of achieving lifestyle goals
- The most effective goal setting should be conducted between the 25th and 30th of each month, for the upcoming month.

⮕ Frontline Profit Machine = Performance Potential

Get ready, set, launch your sales transformation system, keep going, be unwavering in your commitment, believe in your mission, and stick to the program and the Khoury Performance Equation.

> "You cannot change your situation overnight, but you can change your direction overnight."
> — Jim Rohn

Be the leader you can be and fight fiercely against rationalizations: your future true potential has very little to do with where you are now. You will not achieve what some may say are "impossible" results if you do not aspire to them and believe in your ability to achieve them.

If you apply a fraction of what I have talked about in this book, you will see an incredible return on investment. But is that all you really want, a good ROI?

The purpose here is not just for a mere lift of the numbers. The ultimate objective is to create The Right Environment to be able to bring in The Right Fit that can then implement The Right Action. The strategy is to form and sculpt a *Frontline Profit Machine* and to go for it all, to go for your truly deserved performance potential.

The plan is proven the KPE System is here. Regardless of your position within your organization you have the power and the influence to make a difference for yourself, your team, and your business. The choice is yours. If you have gotten this far, I am betting you have made the right choice.

KHOURY KEY TAKEAWAYS
CHAPTER 9

A peak performance culture may be envisioned at a high level but it is built locally.

NO-BULL KNOW HOW!

Effective sales management can be distilled into the following three areas: Firing, hiring, and inspiring.

Firing: *Holding the team accountable provides the biggest opportunity for impact. Address this area through:*

- ✔ The Profit Contribution Report, which crystallizes all the numbers you need to help guide your sales management plan
- ✔ Critical Care, which is an "urgency" program that provides recurrent training for low producers to "get up" or "get out"

Hiring: *The fastest way to achieve your goals is through the right people.*

- ✔ Understand the impact of the transformation performance gap.
- ✔ Move from a passive to a proactive recruitment strategy.
- ✔ Understand the interdependency of the KPE and its influence on recruiting.

Inspiring: *Make it happen through a set of actions that help consistent implementation.*

- ✔ Apply the same principles of the *The Right Action* to get your managers to implement and facilitate a positive and supportive culture. This then has to happen at all levels of management.

Understand and appreciate the following set of sales management tools that have impact on morale and consistent application.

- ✔ Presence on the sales floor
- ✔ Daily game plans as a motivation and communication tool
- ✔ Consistent fine-tuning of the right incentive plans for all levels
- ✔ *Performance-based scheduling*—placing the top sales producers at the top volume locations at the busiest times
- ✔ Setting written monthly goals and recognizing everyone who achieves them

BANKING ON IT!

Apply these proven principles for a win-win outcome; your customers will thank you and your employees will appreciate you. The ability to influence people positively and businesses financially is the optimum career place to be. *You can bank on it!*

INDEX